Helping Yourself with E.S.P.

Also by the Author:

Helping Yourself with Psycho-Cosmic Power

Helping Yourself with White Witchcraft

Miracle Spiritology

The Miraculous Laws of Universal Dynamics

REVISED AND EXPANDED

Helping Yourself with E.S.P.

AL G. MANNING, D.D.

REWARD BOOKS

REWARD BOOKS
An imprint of Prentice Hall Press
A member of Penguin Putnam Inc.
375 Hudson Street
New York, New York 10014
www.penguinputnam.com

Library of Congress Cataloging-in-Publication Data

Manning, Al G.
     Helping yourself with E.S.P. / Al G. Manning. —2nd ed.
       p. cm.
     Includes index.
     ISBN 0-7352-0124-2 (pbk.)
     1. Extrasensory perception. I. Title. II. Title: Helping yourself with
extrasensory perception.
BF1321.M35 1999
133.8—dc21   99-34453
                                                           CIP

Printed in the United States of America

10 9 8 7 6 5 4

To my wife and divine companion
Virginia

How This Book Can Benefit You

Everyone dreams of riches, fame, power, and love. Some people's dreams burst into reality as if brought to fruition in another dimension—while other's come to naught! *The fulfillment of your hopes and dreams is not a matter of chance.* Success in any undertaking is a result of the proper use of natural law. And the natural laws work whether our scientists have discovered them or not!

Men traveled over the water in boats for hundreds of years before Archimedes brought forth the concept of displacement of liquids which makes it possible for a boat to stay on the water. And in this modern world, some enlightened souls are using laws of the mind to achieve their hearts' desires—even though science is still unable to explain it.

How E.S.P. can enrich your life

YOU can learn to experience another dimension of life through *extrasensory perception* (E.S.P.). This unfoldment will bring new meaning and purpose to all areas of your existence. Yes, you can use it to gain health, wealth, power, true love, fame, or anything else you may desire. But its greatest value lies in the change it is certain to bring in your understanding of life. There are depths of meaning and experience far beyond the average man's imagination. The following pages will show you how to develop your extrasensory powers and use them to attain a new understanding and the ability to make your dreams come true.

Wonderfully positive experiences occur in the lives of normal people all over the world—every day. Many are spontaneous, but others happen because some of us are learning the elementary laws of another dimension. Your neighbor may be *working* the same natural laws that brought an ancient prophet to flatly state:

"He will give His angels charge over you, to guard you in all of your ways. They will bear you up in their hands, lest you strike even your foot upon a stone."

This is not an idle dream of some starry-eyed mystic. It is a statement of *UNIVERSAL LAW THAT WILL WORK FOR YOU!*

Why this book is so easy to use

This book is not intended to be "scientific" or "scholarly." It is designed for your use as a tool—to enable you to attain your heart's desires, and more besides! The examples used are from the ordinary lives of normal people. Most of them were obtained from individuals who were eager to share their experiences with others in the hope of bringing upliftment to all mankind. Many came from friends whose integrity is, to me, absolutely beyond question. There may be no incontrovertible "scientific proof" for any of these experiences—but they happened, and lives were enriched as a result!

We start with the assumption that you have never recognized a psychic experience in your own life. This puts you on the same footing with me when I first looked into the confusion of ideas about the next dimension. Then we will *demonstrate to you* that you already have some degree of E.S.P. which you should be using every day. Next we set up a *positive program for your development* of ever-increasing E.S.P. All this is in the first chapter.

The remaining chapters develop the fine points of *application* of your new abilities to each major area of your life. No special talents or aptitudes are required. Nature endowed you at birth with all the necessary tools. Happiness, health, riches, friendship, peace of mind, love, and fulfillment are yours already. This book is designed to show you how to realize your birthright, and attain all these things, now!

Contents

chapter 4

How to Use E.S.P. to Gain Riches in Ever-Increasing Abundance. 67

chapter 5

How to Use E.S.P. to Build a Dynamic Personality That Attracts the Right People. . . . 81

chapter 6

How to Find the Strength
to Face Any Crisis. 93

chapter 7

How E.S.P. Can Reveal Your
True Reason for Living 107

chapter 8

How E.S.P. Can Insure the Success of Your Every Undertaking 119

chapter 9

How to Use E.S.P. to Establish a Personal Relationship with God. 129

chapter 10

How to Use Advanced Psychic Phenomena for E.S.P. 143

chapter 11

How to Insure Your New Growth 169

afterword

Major Problem-Solving to Start a Fresh New Life with E.S.P. 177

how to Develop Your E.S.P.

An old man comes slowly down the street, tapping a white cane to guide his way. Your heart must go out to him in compassion. You have a tremendous advantage over him—you can see, but he can't!

Let's stop and think for a moment. A person with well-developed powers of E.S.P. has much the same advantage over the average man that you have over the blind man. Look at this natural occurrence:

"Al, I couldn't tell just anyone about this," the voice on my telephone blurted, "but I know you'll understand. I was coming about sixty-five miles an hour on the Pasadena Freeway this afternoon, lost in thought. About a mile before the big blind curve I saw a vision of a terrible accident with automobiles blocking the two left lanes. The scene was so vivid in my mind that I simply had to slow down. I coasted to about forty and moved over into the right-hand lane as I rounded the curve. Sure enough, there was the accident exactly as I had seen it! If it weren't for the vision, I'd have ploughed right into those wrecked cars, and I'd be in the hospital or the morgue right now."

This is a simple example of a helpful psychic phenomenon. We will look at many more as we explore practical meth-

1

ods of harnessing this great realm of the unknown. But is the psychic realm really so unknown to you?

You have already experienced many psychic phenomena

Where did your last idea come from? Where did it exist? What is its reality? Its substance? An idea is an intangible substance, a psychic phenomenon! It is an object in that fantastic realm which men call mind, or sometimes even soul. The actual process of thought is not completely understood by medical people, psychologists, or even philosophers; yet it is the means by which they ply their trades, and the means by which we all comprehend the many experiences of life.

Now you are properly introduced to the world of psychic phenomena. You can't say you have never had a *psychic experience,* because your very act of entertaining the idea is one! There are many uncommon or miraculous psychic experiences, but that is only a matter of degree. The psychic, or intangible, side of life is experienced by every living human, every day of his life, and we will do well to spend some time examining its many mysteries.

Legend tells us that Sir Isaac Newton sat under a tree contemplating a mystery. When an apple fell and hit him on the head, it supplied the missing stimulus. There was a moment of contact with reality, and Newton expounded the law of gravity. Similarly, Archimedes is said to have jumped out of the bathtub shouting, "Eureka!" upon subconsciously solving a problem. His contribution was the principle of displacement of water by immersed objects, which paved the way for the floating hunks of steel we call modern ships.

History records both events as milestones in science's march toward understanding our universe. The principles seem obvious today, but only after some mind accomplished the original thinking. All progress is a series of steps best described as the unfoldment of an idea, so in a very real sense, *all progress is a result of the psychic*. This means that the psychic is a sure *means to improve your whole life*.

Your five steps to personal success and greatness

A little self-contemplation will prepare us for the simple five-step path to personal success and greatness. Let's pause for a brief look at the miracle that is *you*. You are much more than the little pile of chemicals which comprise your physical body. A very real part of you can visit Paris, Sydney, Venus, or the moon while your physical body reclines comfortably in the easy chair in your own living room. You are capable of heights of ecstasy and depths of despondency not experienced by any other species of earth creature, and yet you know less about yourself than about the automobile which transports your body from place to place.

Modern man is a fantastic paradox of wasted potential and pathetic ignorance, boundless love and tender compassion, desolate insecurity and murderous frustration, mental agility and physical adaptability—all embarked on the journey of life toward he knows not where!

We squander vast amounts of energy seeking *things*. Automobiles, television sets, new furniture, and fancy clothes may bring us creature comforts, but they can never deliver that precious intangible we call inner satisfaction. Your deepest inner hungers can be fed only by *your personal experience of the miracle* which means your inner self. Then you can handle the physical world easily. It is exactly as Jesus taught it, all those years ago: *Seek ye first the kingdom of God, and his righteousness; and all these things shall be added unto you.* (Matt. 6:33)

And where did the Master say to look for it? Within yourself, of course! It's hard to argue with a Man who demonstrated so much spirituality along with so many varieties of E.S.P., so let's consider His advice instead. Let this set the tone for our approach to the five-step path to personal success and greatness. Briefly stated, the five steps are:

1. Increase your awareness of yourself and the world around you.

2. Recognize your present psychic strengths and potentials.

3. Use regular exercises to develop your E.S.P.

4. Learn to contact powers greater than yourself for guidance and help.

5. Apply your E.S.P. to improve and enrich every department of your life.

We will go into the first three steps in detail in the balance of this chapter. Since the fourth step is an application of what you will learn from the first three, it will be covered in Chapter 2. Then we will devote the rest of our space to the details of application for the enrichment of each area of your life, and to explanations of the wonderfully positive results you can obtain.

How to increase your awareness of yourself and the world around you

The owner of a small service company was so wrapped up in his business problems that he could think of nothing else. Any conversation of a cultural or purely social nature made him quite uncomfortable. He developed the habit of interrupting everyone with lengthy discourses on the problems of his daily business operations. Thus, he effectively prevented any possible broadening of his personality or outlook. Because he shut out everything he might have had in common with them, he lost his wife and family. He wound up with not one friend who wasn't some sort of business necessity. His company grew, and the business world might call him a success; but he died a lonely, broken man.

How can you have the business or professional success you desire, but avoid the pitfall this man fell into? Or is it possible at all? Of course it is! But it requires the sincere application of yourself to the development of our first tool. We will call it *relaxed awareness.*

Much study and practice will be necessary to build your relaxed awareness, but the rewards are great. This is one of the most useful of all mental disciplines. Each of us has two aspects of mind: the conscious, reasoning part which is much like a computer; and the subconscious part which can be your contact with the accumulated wisdom of the ages. Your relaxed awareness will grow out of the increasing confidence in your ability to cope with life. You gain it by learning to assign each of your problems to the right part of your mind for solution.

Today's computers are being used to solve the most complex problems of deductive reasoning. They can even be programmed to make routine management decisions, but only of a *deductive* nature. Your conscious mind is quite like a computer and should be accepted as such. When a computer receives a problem, all the elements necessary for a solution must be present or it will light up the tilt and reject the query pending the required additional inputs. But how about people? When we encounter a problem but don't have all the necessary data, we become anxious or frustrated! Why? Because we are trying to use the wrong mental machine.

It is only the power of your subconscious which sets you apart as more valuable than a computer. The subconscious is your source of the missing data for the solution of any problem, if you will but learn to *use it.* Next time you are faced with a problem and your reasoning mind can't arrive at a good answer, don't allow anxiety to rob you of your peace of mind. Instead, turn it over to the subconscious and trust your inner self to deliver help at the right time. Meanwhile, you can continue to genuinely participate in each moment of life. You will find it no longer necessary to grunt in response to your spouse or child while you are absorbed in anxious thought. You can enjoy your family and friends and get a better solution to the problem as well. A little further along we will present a simple technique for concentration to turn over your knotty problems to the subconscious mind for certain and trustworthy solutions, but first we need to examine some of your areas of psychic potential as outlined below.

Seven simple tests for your special psychic abilities

There are many simple experiences which our materialistic culture has taught us to shrug off as meaningless or sheer coincidence. They are *real psychic experiences,* and they can serve as definite clues to your own areas of special psychic aptitude. All of us are involved in some of these at least once in awhile. How often do you experience one of these?

1. HUNCHES

You get a feeling about some present or future occurrence, and it is strong enough that you feel impelled to remark, "I have a hunch that . . ." Sure enough, it turns out that you were right. (Hunches are generally associated with clairsentience or intuition.)

2. FEEL SOMEONE'S EYES

While in a public place, you suddenly feel someone looking at you. When you turn around, you meet the other's gaze and know you were right. (This is also most often a form of clairsentience.)

3. PROPHETIC DREAMS

Last night you dreamed that Aunt Susie came to visit you. Then this morning you received a letter saying that she will arrive on Monday. Or take any dream that turns out to be substantially fulfilled shortly afterward. (This is commonly called precognition.)

4. YOU'VE BEEN THERE BEFORE

While visiting some new place, you have a funny feeling you have been there before. You somehow seem to know what type of building will appear as you round the next corner; or perhaps you know exactly the words your companion will use to describe a scene or another person. (This could be clairsentience, precognition, or possibly a previous astral experience.)

5. MENTAL PICTURES OR INNER VOICES

While sitting quietly with your eyes open or closed, you see a picture of a scene or a person on the screen of your inner vision. Or you hear someone whisper your name or a short phrase, but you are quite alone. (This would be simple clairvoyance or clairaudience.)

6. TELEPHONE COINCIDENCE

You want to call up a friend or relative, but while you are still looking for the number, your telephone rings and it is that person calling you. If this has happened to you more than once, either as the one about to make the call or the one actually calling, forget about coincidence. This is a definite manifestation of telepathy.

7. WOMAN'S INTUITION

The thing called woman's intuition is just as common to men as to women, though men are not so apt to admit it. If you have ever considered using a term like this to explain how you knew something, you admit that you have definite psychic aptitude.

I feel completely safe in saying that everyone who reads this book has had many such experiences. If you feel you have not, it is undoubtedly a matter of awareness. We have been trained since childhood to ignore such things or shrug them off as coincidence. Start looking for it, and within one short week you will notice at least three such experiences.

These simple psychic experiences are important! They can be the beginning of a richer and more meaningful life for *you*. They are your key to the doorway to ever-increasing health, wealth, happiness, and spiritual progress. Even if you feel you failed all seven psychic tests, there is no reason to be discouraged. Psychic ability is an inherent part of *every* human being, and like the ability to read, it can be learned at any age. Naturally some people will develop into better psychics than others, just as some learn to read with greater speed and retention than others. But the advantages of a reader over a nonreader are quite similar in quality to those of one who consciously uses the psychic over one who does not.

There is an old truism, "That which you seek is seeking you." In modern language we might put it, the application of your interest tends to attract its subject. Begin *now* to seek manifestation of the psychic in your daily experience. As you progress, we will show you how to build it into a working tool that is *useful in all areas of your life.*

Your five senses are your link to the psychic

Science recognizes five basic senses, or means by which individuals perceive conditions and events in the world around us. They are named sight, hearing, touch, taste, and smell. However, they are not as specific and concrete as we might first think There is a tremendous variation in the degree of each sense as demonstrated by different individuals. Glasses and hearing aids bear constant testimony to our many variations of less-than-normal sight and hearing, but there are also cases of exceptionally keen degrees of these key receptors.

The senses are your mind's basic method of perceiving the objective world. Thus they are a link between the concrete–physical and the subjective–psychic realm. The intensity or effectiveness of this link varies not only from individual to individual, but within the same person as a function of health, inclination, and attention. We all know someone who is quite hard of hearing except when you softly speak something you don't want that person to hear.

His teacher reported that young Johnny seemed to be hard of hearing. She regularly had to call him two or three times to get his attention. Subsequent tests revealed that his hearing was completely normal, but his intelligence level was above the work of the class, and he daydreamed out of sheer boredom. A more challenging class and increased parental interest removed the problem in less than three weeks.

Some degree of the same lack of awareness exhibited by the unchallenged child is found in each of us. We often fail to observe events in our immediate vicinity because we "couldn't care less." Conscious development of the power to regularly control and direct your interest will add many degrees to your livingness, and to your ability to recall important facts and events you previously would not have even noticed. This power is most accurately labeled *concentration.*

How to develop the art of concentration

Concentration is an art, like painting or playing a musical instrument. Your inherent ability must be developed by regular practice and application of yourself to a program graduated in difficulty to bring you from a point of amorphous potential to a peak of professional skill. The usefulness of a super ability to concentrate obviously extends to every area of your life, and it is certainly worth a little effort to achieve.

Most people actually miss about three quarters of life because they don't observe what they think they see. Listen to three disinterested witnesses of an automobile accident as they give their accounts of the details. Generally you would think they must be talking about events that took place at widely different times and places because of the conflicting details. The simple ability to accurately observe and recall detail is a manifestation of applied concentration. Let's begin with an exercise to develop yours:

Look around the house and find an old wooden pencil. Examine it carefully and make a list of everything you observe about it. Finish your own list before you compare it with the one below.

Details of an old wooden pencil:

A. Colors

   1. Point—dark gray graphite

   2. Wooden part of point—many shades of brown and gray

   3. Shaft—painted yellow-orange, chipped here and there with bare wood showing through

   4. Lettering—some black and more by indentations in the painted finish

   5. Metal eraser holder—brass with two red stripes around it

   6. Eraser—pearly pink with smudges of black and gray

B. Shapes

   1. Tip of point—rounded

   2. Point—conical

   3. Shaft—hexagonal, about 5 inches long

   4. Eraser holder—cylindrical, but ribbed and perforated

   5. Eraser—cylindrical, but worn to many shapes of flatness and little corners

C. Materials

   1. Graphite

   2. Wood

   3. Paint—yellow-orange and black

   4. Brass

   5. Red anodized material on the stripe

      6. Rubber

      7. Flecks of dirt

  D. Distinguishing Features

      1. Trademark

      2. Brand name and number

      3. Lead hardness—#3

      4. Made in USA

      5. Process—"Chemi-sealed"

      6. Quality-control number 316325

      7. Many dents and teeth marks

      8. Point—very dull

  E. Potential Uses

      1. Writing

      2. Erasing

      3. Drawing

      4. Weapon (stab or scratch)

      5. Wedge or shim

      6. Window prop

      7. Lever

      8. Fuel (the wood)

      9. Lubricant (the graphite)

    10. Hair roller

    11. Spool for string or thread

    12. Stirring rod

    13. Dipstick for shallow tank

    14. Measuring instrument (length)

    15. Subject of a painting

This list merely scratches the surface, but it was prepared in less than three minutes and it serves to illustrate our point.

Your powers of observation will increase by leaps and bounds as you practice focusing your whole attention on one subject at a time. Practice this exercise on a different object each day for two weeks, and you will be on your way to its mastery. Use simple things at first, like a knife, fork, scissors, mirror, glass, cup, dish, etc. When you think you're good at it, try a flower such as a rose. You should feel that you could fill a whole book with the details of just one rose.

Practice! It is well worth your while. When your concentration is well sharpened by this process, you are ready to apply it to solving real-life problems.

How to solve all your problems through concentration and meditation

Somewhere in the psychic realms there exists a creative solution to your every problem. You can tune in on it, and manifest harmonious progress by a combination of concentration and meditation. The preliminary process is applied concentration. By using the powers of concentration you have just developed, clearly analyze and define your problem; that is the purpose of your conscious mind. Then you are ready to use that part of your being which makes you better than a computer.

You will find that your applied concentration reveals the solution to the majority of your problems with no further effort. The remaining ones, being clearly defined, now lack only the creative idea that leads to their mastery. In years gone by, such creative solutions were often chalked up to Yankee ingenuity. *You* are endowed with an endless fountain of this Yankee ingenuity; it is only necessary to open the valve and let it flow into your experience.

The process of turning on your mental tap is best called *meditation.* Sit quietly alone, and calmly review your analysis of the problem. Next, talk to your own subconscious as if it were another person. Say something like: "O.K., Subconscious, I know you are the source of all creative ideas. Let's see how you handle this one." Then relax and wait. If you get no immediate answer, don't be discouraged. Get busy with your routine chores, and your answer will come in an intuitive flash during a moment of mental relaxation.

A man had just lost $100,000 in a disastrous used car venture. He talked it over with his subconscious like this: "Look here, Subconscious, because of this big loss, I can make $100,000 tax free in the next few years. What are we going to do about it?" For two days nothing happened, but he didn't worry. There were plenty of tasks involved with winding up his ill-fated venture, and he kept busy with them. On the morning of the third day he awakened with a simple chemical formula running around in his head. By noon it had jelled into a novel process for making a widely used product, so he called up an old acquaintance who arranged the necessary financing. The result? In just 18 months he had his $100,000 back and half of a prosperous business as well.

The real secret of using the meditative art of problem solving lies in the approach of the man in our example. He didn't cry over his loss and wallow in self-pity. Rather, he adopted the most positive outlook. Here was not a personal catastrophe, but a beautiful opportunity to make a lot of money, tax free! Anxiety or despondency will prevent your subconscious from delivering the goods; but a positive, optimistic attitude absolutely guarantees success. Never accept anxiety and frustration as a way of life. Use the meditative process to clear away the pressures by solving all your problems. Begin to enjoy every moment of life, *now!*

We learn about E.S.P. from the Orient

With our materialistic pressures of life relieved, we are ready to look deeper into the realm of E.S.P. From centuries before the time of Christ, men of the Orient have been teaching the development of the psychic senses. It will help us to examine some of these ancient Eastern teachings. There are practical uses for many of them in our Western world today.

Basically the great Eastern teachers look upon man as a spirit expressing through a soul which uses, among other vehicles, a physical body. This physical body is understood to be a beast of burden, like a horse, which provides transportation for the soul on the earth plane, even as the mind provides a means of expression in the thought realms. The physical senses are tools of the physical body, and the psychic senses are tools of the finer body of light, which is most often called the *astral body*.

Under proper conditions the astral body, which contains the seat of consciousness, can be separated from the physical body and travel independently for great distances. The energy, and the very life, of the physical body comes to it through the astral vehicle which connects with the physical through the sympathetic nervous system. Thus the astral self is associated with the emotional part of your being. If you stop to think about it, energy flow through your body is always the result of emotion. There is an energy of love, hate, enthusiasm, pride, joy, jealousy, greed, and the like.

Each one of us has experienced the spark of enthusiasm that drives fatigue out of the body and equips it to enjoy a few lines of bowling or rubbers of bridge after a truly hard day's work. This is only one of many indications that the Eastern masters know a lot more than our modern culture is willing to admit. We will omit much of the detail of their teachings, examining only the bare essentials necessary to a useful understanding. From our standpoint, the main question is: If there really is an *astral body,* can we learn to make conscious, practical use of it in our daily lives? And though many may quarrel with the terminology, we will find the answer to be a definite *yes!*

The mechanics of psychic sensation— psychic centers

By a process analogous to the transmission of electricity, the physical body is supplied with light-energy through the sympathetic nervous system. A brief review of the household use of electricity will aid our understanding. For purposes of economy, electricity is transmitted from the generating station at relatively high voltages, then it is converted to the safer energy we use in our homes by means of step-down transformers. The energy supplied to most homes comes in at 115 volts, but for many applications, such as your doorbell, other step-down transformers are required to reduce the voltage to the 6 volts or 12 volts used by the more delicate apparatus.

The light-energy is transmitted within your body-house by the nervous system. Each nerve is like an electric wire in your house, and the nerve centers are like the secondary coils of a transformer. Then where are the primary coils? They are in your *astral* counterpart. Consequently, each ganglion or nerve center in your body is also a psychic center, and these are the suppliers of the vital energy which is the life of your body.

Because pain is a form of energy, we see that it is through the astral body that we experience the sensation of pain. When the astral is separated from the physical body, there is no feeling of any kind left in the physical. With this little bit of background, you can readily understand the mechanics of psychic sensation and learn to use it in almost the same way you learned to coordinate your eyes and intellect in the process of reading. There is a special form of yoga used by our Eastern friends to gain conscious control over each individual muscle in their bodies, and another yoga used to attain similar control over the many psychic centers. These disciplines represent truly magnificent attainments, but they are of only academic interest to us. Our purpose is to improve your life in our modern Western civilization; and we are interested only in that which specifically helps us *here* and in the reasonably near *now*. For our practical approach we need consider only seven major psychic centers.

Your seven most important psychic centers

For those who are interested in more detail, a trip to your public library to look up some topics like *chakra, Ida, pingala, sushumna,* or the *fire of the kundalini* should provide much interesting reading. But we will confine this discussion to the following centers:

1. The *Root Center* is located at the base of the spine. It is associated with the organs of reproduction, and thus with physical creativity of all kinds. It provides much of the energy that we call "get up and go" or drive in union with the two other lower centers.

2. The *Spleen Center* is located along the spine in the area of the spleen. It is an energy purifier and a transformer of low-vibration energy to higher-vibration energy. As the middleman of the lower three centers, one of its major functions is coordinating and balancing the activity of its immediate neighbors.

3. The *Solar Plexus Center* is located in the area of the navel or the physical solar plexus. This is the center most sensitive to the animal emotions, and is recognized by modern psychology when it speaks of gut-level discussions. All the negative emotions, such as fear, hate, anxiety, lust, and despair, hit us in the gut, causing butterflies, knots, indigestion, or ulcers. This is an amazingly sensitive receiving station for picking up the lower emotions in other people.

4. The *Heart Center* is located in the area of the physical heart. This is the middle center, representing the balance between the higher mental centers and the lower physical centers. It is the transformer which brings the positive emotions of love, compassion, and enthusiasm into usable energy on the physical plane. Love is the perfect balance between the heat of the lower physical drives and the intellectual cold of the higher centers. Of course, all the centers are necessary to the total functioning of a complete spiritual being.

5. The *Throat Center* is located in the region of the thyroid gland. It is the lower center of the upper three, and is associated with creativity like its counterpart, the root center. But

this creativity is of a higher abstract nature which includes the arts, literature, music, and science.

6. The *Brow Center* is located behind and slightly above the eyes, in the region of the pituitary gland. Like its spleen center counterpart, it is important particularly in purifying and balancing the energies flowing between its immediate neighbors. The brow center is symbolized by a jewel worn near the center of the forehead, and it is often called the gateway to illumination because it is our means of activating the highest center.

7. The *Crown Center* is located near the top of the head in the region of the pineal gland. It is no accident that the occult lore of the ages has branded the pineal gland the seat of psychic ability and the instrument of spiritual attainment. The spiritual power flowing through a fully functioning crown center is wonderful beyond finite belief, yet it brings a distinctly personal relationship with God and all His creation. In a very real sense, the purpose of this book is to help you develop this center as your means to certain accomplishment of any goal.

A basic exercise to develop your E.S.P.

As we begin work to increase the activity of your psychic body, it is extremely important that we stress simple *balance*. The Bible insists that you are created in the image and likeness of God. Now this doesn't mean that God has to look like a physical man! But it does mean that, like God, *you are a whole being.* You are a composite whole, made up of physical, emotional–psychic, mental, and spiritual aspects. You attain maximum effectiveness only when all of your parts are working together. On a football team the guard and tackle positions are not the glamour spots. They may be noticed by the average fan only when they miss an important block or tackle, but their devoted performance is the mainstay of the team. Similarly, some spiritual leaders forget the value of the physical body and insist on its subjugation, but without the physical body we are helpless to manifest on this earth. We must bring our *whole being* along on a program of balanced development. True, we must learn to control the wonderful horse that is our physical body, but the stronger the horse, the better the ride.

Here, then, is our first psychic exercise designed to promote a balanced increase in your overall psychic activity:

Sit or stretch out comfortably where you will not be disturbed. Relax your body and quiet your mind as much as possible. Now concentrate on your *root center.* Try to imagine that all of your consciousness exists at that one spot, that all your thought, feeling, and sensation are centered there. Soon you will feel a warm tingling sensation near the base of your spine. As you begin to feel this psychic response, imagine a whirling circle of flame ever growing and increasing its speed of rotation while stepping up the power of the center.

Now direct this energy to your *spleen center,* causing it to tingle and itself become a vortex of whirling flame. Transfer all your attention to the spleen center, and imagine the flame growing and rotating faster and faster. Feel the increased power flowing through this center! Now direct this energy to your *solar plexus center* and repeat the whole process. Intensify the flame and lift it, repeating all the steps, in turn, to the *heart, throat, brow,* and finally the *crown center.* When you feel your crown center tingling with all the energy you can bring to it, make the following statement:

"I seek to promote the growth of my overall being through the stimulation of my psychic senses. This is good for me and I know that my subconscious self is cooperating in every way. I sit in the silence awaiting the voice of my inner self."

Then just sit quietly for a few minutes. You may receive nothing at first, or you may be amazed at the immediate results. But you are definitely progressing! Either way, continue the exercise daily if possible, but at least three times a week.

Understand that you are stimulating the flow of the psychic energies throughout your body as you continue the exercise. If some part of your body is not functioning at peak efficiency, you can help it by directing the psychic energies you are summoning to yourself from the universe. As you consciously bring each center to its maximum vibratory rate, direct its healing force to your afflicted part before transferring your attention to the next higher center. Thus you bathe the limb or organ with healing energy of seven different rates of vibration, and *it must be improved!*

One big word of caution is in order here. There is a potential danger from habitual incomplete use of this exercise! If you regularly fall asleep or quit in the middle, you will be developing your lower centers more rapidly than the balancing upper centers. Such an imbalanced development could lead to an overemphasis of the sex drive or other strictly material urges. Of course, sex is beautiful, and material things are delightful; but without the complementary esthetic and spiritual experiences, life is hollow and empty. Health is not of the physical only! It is a natural by-product of mental–psychic and spiritual growth along a balanced path. All parts of life are equally important, and none should be neglected. As you use this exercise, apply special emphasis to those centers which seem to correspond to your weaker departments. Strive for balanced growth and you will achieve health, prosperity, and happiness beyond your most cherished dreams.

How to develop clairvoyance

As my telephone rang I closed my eyes and got a mental picture of a rabbit, the symbol I had previously associated with one particular friend. So I reached for the receiver and answered, "Hello, Eddie, how are you?"

You can easily imagine his reaction. You will find it lots of fun to amaze your friends with simple demonstrations like this. As an interesting little sidelight, you will be fascinated by the resemblance of your symbols to important personality traits of your victims.

Almost everybody does some mental imaging. For instance: When you hear the word *apple*, what do you see? How about *purple*? Or *horse*? Some years ago I still believed I was a non-imager. I took some consolation in the knowledge that words like love, courage, or beauty cannot be seen by mental imaging. In my sour grapes, I decided that my abstract thinking must be superior to that of an imager because my mind was not cluttered with a lot of pictures. But that is utter nonsense! Everyone sees a mental picture of some sort once in awhile and that is all that is necessary.

Clairvoyance is nothing more than the reception of mental images with some recognition of their meaning. Basically, you develop clairvoyance by learning to pay attention to something that has always been with you. Try it now! Close your eyes and stare at the patterns you see. Like a child watching a cloud formation, use your imagination to decide what it is and what it may mean. Form your thoughts into words, preferably spoken aloud, and as you vocalize them, your image will tend to focus itself and confirm the accuracy of your speculation.

Our next exercise concerns telling time. Next time you wonder what time it is, stop before looking at your watch. Close your eyes and picture a large white clock face before you. Now look at the hands and read the time. If it checks with your watch, you have produced an excellent demonstration of clairvoyance. Practice is the major ingredient for successful development of this very useful faculty.

Another good exercise is to use clairvoyance to locate missing articles. Instead of thrashing around the house looking for your scissors or pen, close your eyes and visualize it, carefully noting its surroundings. When you walk to it, there where you saw it, you are demonstrating another practical application of clairvoyance.

Don't become discouraged if you are not highly successful with each exercise in the beginning. The basic exercise to activate your psychic centers will work to improve all of your faculties. Persistence and practice will produce startling results in a few short weeks.

Here is another phase of clairvoyance that can be very fruitful. During your quiet, relaxed moments, you will often receive a mental picture with no apparent cause. Learn to pay attention! Recognize these pictures as messages from the great subconscious domain and contemplate their significance. The subconscious speaks to us in symbols, but speak it does, and much helpful information and insight can be obtained in this manner. There is literally a whole new world hidden beneath the threshold of our course, normal consciousness, and it has countless practical uses. The key to entering this exciting place is simply to become alert and sensitive to the many little things we have ignored or shrugged off in the past. Let's turn now to another phase of E.S.P. that is even more accessible to rapid development.

How to develop clairsentience

Clairsentience is the extension of your consciousness by the vehicle of *feeling.* A businessman had scheduled the 8 P.M. flight from Los Angeles to San Francisco because it suited his timetable perfectly. On this particular morning he awakened with an uneasy feeling that he should take an earlier flight, even if it meant canceling his late afternoon appointments. As the day wore on, the feeling became so strong that he "gave in to it" and took the 6 P.M. plane. Next morning at breakfast his paper carried the story of the tragic crash of the 8 P.M. flight. Clairsentience had clearly saved his life.

At some time or other, *everyone* has experienced an unexplainable feeling of uneasiness. This *feeling* is a manifestation of *your* clairsentience. Certainly you have at least one acquaintance whose very presence makes you uncomfortable, and others with whom you instinctively relax. This is an example of elementary clairsentience, but it can also be the basis of a good exercise for further development. Start paying attention to that *feeling!* Next time you get a letter or phone call, observe your feeling about it first. See if you can tell what the subject matter will be and who is trying to reach you before you open the letter or answer the phone.

Your increasing awareness of the little things taking place within and around you will lead to accomplishments and the unfolding of talents beyond anything you can presently imagine. We must hammer away at the concept of *paying attention* to those little feelings and images that were always there, but have regularly been ignored.

The feeling that "I've been here before," as you enter a place for the first time, is generally another manifestation of clairsentience. That feeling is most often produced by our accidentally tuning in to the subconscious vibrational patterns of the new place and finding that they coincide with strong feelings in our memory. We feel that we have been there before because we have previously experienced feelings like those being picked up. There may be other instances when you have "been there before" in your astral body, but we will come to that discussion in a later chapter.

You can learn many things about any place you visit by purposely tuning in to subconscious feelings that are ever present in its atmosphere. You tune in simply by focusing your attention on the feelings which are impinging upon you from your surroundings. Have those who lived here been generally happy or sad? Which way do you feel as you mentally ask the question? That is your answer, unless your personal feelings have crowded out the truth. You can *feel* a generally sound answer to almost any question you would expect the place to hold in its memory.

Here is an exercise close to home. How often do you instinctively sense the mood of your spouse or a good friend? That is clearly clairsentience! You can easily improve your ability to sense another's mood by applying more of yourself to it. Let your conscious mind be temporarily pushed aside by the incoming feelings. *Become* the other person for an instant; *feel* his feelings and *think* his thoughts, not as yourself, but as the other person; then bring the impressions back into sharp mental focus. This can be a doubly good exercise. It helps develop your clairsentience and improves your human relations as well.

Common sense will tell you that clenching your teeth, grunting, or anxiously striving will never help you *feel* anything. *Use your relaxed awareness*. It is the key, now and always!

How to listen for the voice of clairaudience

For centuries, poets and clergymen have rambled on about the *still, small voice* that speaks to you in the silence. It can become prattling when the writer is talking about a concept rather than a direct experience. But just because an idea isn't always well presented is not a valid reason to dismiss it as worthless or untrue. There is an allegorical still, small voice which is intuitional and directly related to clairsentience, but there is also a *true voice of clairaudience*.

Did you ever think you heard your name whispered softly in your ear, but when you looked around there was nobody there? If you must answer "no," listen carefully in the future, it will be there. History records an excellent example of guidance and comfort from the voices of clairaudience; and fortunately for us, society is more tolerant today. The voices that led Joan of Arc were real! They stand ready to guide and help you today! You have only to *pay attention*.

We call mental pictures *clairvoyance,* feelings *clairsentience,* and hearing *clairaudience,* but in a larger sense they are all one. They are more likely to manifest in concert with one another than separately. It is the same with the five physical senses; the occasion is rare indeed when one sense is used alone. Taste and smell greatly reinforce one another and so do sight and sound; a television set minus either picture or the sound is much less effective. So it is that all E.S.P. has been poetically called the *sixth sense*. Our goal is to open ourselves to the guidance and inspiration of the great subconscious realm, and the name given to the process is of little consequence.

To develop clairaudience you must sit in the silence and listen! But it would be folly to reject mental pictures or clairsentient impressions while doing so. As you practice the exercise for awakening your psychic centers, and direct your relaxed awareness to the whole of the psychic realm, you will get results. You may notice a buzzing or ringing in your ears as you sit and listen. Accept it with thanks as the beginning of your clairaudience.

You have probably spent years rejecting such ideas. Those old thought patterns may impede your progress but *you will improve daily.* Just as it takes time for an athlete to attain his peak physical condition and develop the skills of his sport, it takes awhile to condition yourself to the ways of the psychic and develop your powers of reception. The help to be gained from the psychic is far more valuable than any gold medal won on the field of athletic competition. You can use it to *achieve any goal,* or *open any door!* The price is always growth and self-development. Where else does paying the price so directly enrich the payer?

How to clear away the blocks to extrasensory development

In the early stages of psychic development we tend to build up blocks to our progress. The three major blocks are:

1. Disbelief.
2. Fear and its consequent tension.
3. Anxiety or just plain overeagerness.

It is important to dissolve these blocks as quickly as you notice their development. To fight them is only to give them strength, but they can be gently dissolved with knowledge and understanding. Let's work on them one by one.

The block of disbelief can rob you of your will to try. It must be dissolved in order to maintain the enthusiasm necessary to success. The great and growing science of parapsychology gives plenty of intellectual credence to E.S.P. We will assume your intellectual acceptance for the moment and consider the religious aspect. The greatest value of the New Testament lies in the Master's challenge and promise: . . . *He that believeth on me, the works that I do shall he do also; and greater works than these shall he do* . . . (John 14:12)

And what are these works? Certainly much of Jesus' life story is involved with demonstrations of E.S.P. There are a good hundred examples of the Master's highly developed E.S.P. in the four gospels. Let's take a brief look at one from each:

Matthew 17:27: *Notwithstanding, lest we should offend them, go thou to the sea, and cast a hook, and take up the first fish that cometh up; and when thou hast opened his mouth, thou shalt find a piece of money: that take, and give unto them for me and thee.* (Clairvoyance and/or materialization of physical substance)

Mark 9:4: *And there appeared unto them Elias with Moses: and they were talking with Jesus.* (Spirit materialization)

Luke 5:22, 23: *But when Jesus perceived their thoughts, he answering said unto them, What reason ye in your hearts? Whether is easier to say, Thy sins be forgiven thee; or to say, Rise up and walk?* (Clairsentience)

John 1:47, 48: *Jesus saw Nathanael coming to him, and saith of him, Behold an Israelite indeed, in whom is no guile. Nathanael saith unto him, Whence knowest thou me? Jesus answered and said unto him, Before that Philip called thee, when thou wast under the fig tree, I saw thee.* (Clairvoyance)

These four illustrative examples were picked for their brevity. There are many longer and more dramatic accounts of Jesus' regular demonstrations of all forms of E.S.P. Remember that he claimed to be not the great exception, but rather a challenging example to all men! Should we break the faith and refuse to follow Him? Reread the Gospels while carefully watching for examples of E.S.P. and let all doubt and disbelief dissolve in your new enlightened understanding.

The block of *fear* can drive your results away. At the moment when we experience our first clear demonstration, many of us feel an almost overwhelming fear of the power of the unknown. This fear tends to drive away any further demonstrations. There are only two solvents for this block. They are knowledge and the familiarity born of broadened experience. It takes real courage to keep on in the face of that formless fear. I freely admit that the hair stood straight out on the back of my neck the first time I was aware of the touch of a being without a physical body. There was an almost overwhelming urge to run! But the conscious mind couldn't answer my next question, "Run where?" So I sat still and enjoyed a wonderful experience. There is nothing to fear but your own thoughts!

Now disbelief has been replaced by understanding, and fear by knowledge and experience; it should all be downhill. It is here, as we recognize the great value and fantastic potential of E.S.P., that most of us get overanxious. We want it all, *now,* with no further work or waiting. So we tense up and try too hard. Nothing is more destructive to your E.S.P.! When you get tense, decide to relax immediately, then help accomplish it with a simple breathing exercise.

Shut your mouth and inhale through your nose. Fill your lungs to capacity and hold your breath while you count slowly to twenty-two. Then exhale slowly through your nose, emptying your lungs as completely as possible. Now immediately inhale through your nose, filling the lungs again. Continue for from three to seven complete breaths until you feel the anxiety abated.

Now practice

On May 8, 1965, Randy Matson became the first human to shot put over 70 feet, just a few short years after Roger Bannister broke the 4-minute mile. How well do you think either of these men did the first time they tried? Success in any worthwhile undertaking is the result of great effort applied in an organized manner. You don't have to become the equivalent of a Matson or a Bannister to bring a good measure of E.S.P. into your life, but you must put forth a reasonable amount of plain old effort. Every moment you spend practicing the exercises will bring its reward of increased proficiency. Then you can turn your attention to the many practical applications of *your ever-growing proficiency.*

POINTS TO REMEMBER

I. The five steps to personal success and greatness:

    A. Increase your awareness.

    B. Recognize your psychic ability.

    C. Develop your E.S.P.

    D. Contact powers greater than yourself.

    E. Apply your E.S.P.

II. Work for relaxed awareness.

III. You already have psychic ability.

IV. Develop your concentration by use of the exercise.

V. Apply concentration and meditation to the solution of any problem.

VI. Man is a spirit expressing through a soul which uses a physical body.

VII. Practice the basic exercise to develop your psychic centers.

VIII. Exercise to develop your clairvoyance, clairsentience, and clairaudience.

IX. Work to dissolve the blocks to your psychic development.

how to
Contact Powers Greater Than Yourself and Get Real Help for Your E.S.P.

If E.S.P. were just a parlor game or something to occupy a few people in ivory towers, we would have no reason to give it our attention. But it has a range of intensely practical applications stretching from finding a lost cuff link or acquiring fame and fortune, to achieving an intimate, personal relationship with the Creator of the universe.

Your place in the universe

Since he first climbed down out of the trees and began to assert his dominion over the earth, man has intuitively sensed a purposeful, creative force underlying the manifestation he calls the Universe. The intricate detail of the atom repeats itself in ever-more complex patterns which stretch into the vast galaxies of outer space. Throughout the great scheme of things, the order and intelligence are so obvious that no thinking individual can shrug it all off as a gigantic accident.

History records many changes in man's understanding of the details which make up our world, but the creative intelligence and power behind it all remains forever unchanged. Most men agree to call this intelligent force *God,* and the seeking of a personal relationship with it *religion.* The plain fact is

you can't go it alone. God is the life and the very substance of
your being, whether you like it or not! You will find life a much
richer experience when you have surrendered your separateness and replaced it with a *living religion.*

Modern psychology confirms the necessity of religion to
our mental health. The brand or denomination is not important;
but if an individual is to be a "whole being," it is essential that
he establish a satisfying relationship with the power he recognizes as God. Religious diversity is good. It provides a channel
of experience and expression for the varied natural inclinations
and aptitudes of the hodgepodge we call mankind. But within
it all there are many threads of essence—common truths and
manifestations—which truly bind the entire species of man to
the loving worship of *one true God,* though they may call Him
(or It) (or even Them) by a thousand different names.

One of these threads is *love.* We find it even in the fiercest
oriental-despot type deities conceived by primitive man. The
deepest experience of God's love is a common meeting place of
all religions. This is the glorious union with everything that is,
which is best described as the mystic experience. We will devote
a whole chapter to "How to Use E.S.P. to Establish a Personal
Relationship with God." But meanwhile we want to look at
another of the threads which bind the many religions into one.

Most of the religious scripture of our world is believed by
its adherents to have come to man directly from God. However, a study of the scriptures themselves reveals that they pur-
port to have come by the intervention of spirit entities on God's
behalf. For instance, the great religion Islam grew out of a
series of mystical conversations between Mohammed and an
entity or entities described at different places in the Koran as
the Spirit, the Holy Spirit, and the Angel Gabriel. Or in the story
of the beginnings of Christianity, right in the first chapter of
Luke, we find:

*And there appeared unto him an angel of the Lord stand-
ing on the right side of the altar of incense. And when Zacharias
saw him, he was troubled and fear fell upon him. But the angel
said unto him, "Fear not, Zacharias: for thy prayer is heard;*

and thy wife Elizabeth shall bear thee a son and thou shalt call his name John." . . . *And Zacharias said unto the angel, "Whereby shall I know this? For I am an old man, and my wife well stricken in years."*

And the angel answering said unto him, "I am Gabriel, that stand in the presence of God; and am sent to speak unto thee, and to show these glad tidings. And behold, thou shalt be dumb, and not able to speak, until the day that these things shall be performed, because thou believest not my words, which shall be fulfilled in their season."

Certainly spirit contact didn't end with the last accepted words of scripture. Down through the ages into the present day, people pray. They pray to the Saints, the Virgin Mary, Jesus of Nazareth, or directly to God; and they *expect to be heard.* By its very definition, any form of prayer is an attempt at spirit contact. Our purpose in this chapter is to unfold your ability to contact those spirit beings who *can* and *will* be of the utmost help to you all the rest of your life. In other words, we will learn *how to be sure of an answer to all our prayers.* We will begin by learning to contact your own higher self.

How to use E.S.P. to contact your higher self

The logical first subject for an attempt at spirit contact is that ever-present entity, your higher self. The ancient occult traditions tell us to begin by purifying the temple. Naturally the temple referred to is your mind–body, even as Jesus referred to His body when He said that He could rebuild the temple in three days. It stands to reason that the higher elements of life will not be attracted to a body which is in a run-down or degraded condition.

Here common sense is the watchword. It isn't necessary to give up any of life's pleasures, but we should avoid overindulgence of all kinds. The healthier the body, the sharper will be its means of perception, both physical and extrasensory. We won't dwell further on purifying your temple except to say that purity of thought is of even more importance than purity of the strictly physical temple. Your response from the spirit realms will always come in harmony with your dominant mood at the time you seek the contact. Let's take care to seek the higher self only after we have cleansed our mind of its collected negative thoughts.

Now find a quiet place where you will not be disturbed and begin to seek the contact. There is a part of your being which already exists on the higher planes of life. It is the seat of all your morality, and a source of inspiration and positive impulses. It is so much higher than what you normally consider to be yourself that it is easier to comprehend if we think of it as a separate personality and give it a name. For many years I have called my higher self "George," but you should pick the name for yours which seems most appropriate for you. For ease of illustration, I will use the name "George" for your higher self in the following exercise:

Relax in your quiet place and fill your mind with thoughts of peace, prosperity, harmony, health, abundance, love, and joy. Briefly run through our basic exercise for psychic development to sharpen your receptivity (see Chapter 1). Then call George by name, saying something like: "George, we have been together for a long time. Now I am ready to get better acquainted. What should I be learning from you, now?"

Expect an answer through one or more of your rapidly developing channels of E.S.P. No one can describe the thrill of that first contact no matter how slight it may seem later. With a little patience *you will get your response!* You can talk over all your problems with George, and get surprisingly helpful answers. Remember, the response doesn't have to come in a loud voice or a thunderclap. Your awareness of the little things and understanding of their meaning is the secret of successful reception. Practice regularly, and *pay attention!* Ask George to set the mental tone for each day before you get out of bed in the morning. This contact is the most basic, and it is certainly worth all the effort necessary to establish it.

How to receive guidance and help from our "elders" in the next dimension

Again let's start our approach with a peek at the occult lore of the ages. Throughout the mass of occult literature there runs the thread of the concept of the Divine Hierarchy. This Divine Hierarchy is said to be an organization of members of the spirit world, headed by the *ascended masters* and staffed with many devoted workers whose last earth lives were spent in study and earnest spiritual service to mankind. The express purpose of this organization is the upliftment of mankind and the furthering of its progress or evolution along spiritual lines.

Contact with the Hierarchy can be most beneficial along material as well as spiritual paths. When you have identified your own teacher and clearly established your contact, you can expect tangible help of any sort you need. In the next section we will look closely at several specific examples of help in finding a better job, a perfect spouse, and a whole new path of spiritual unfoldment; but first we will begin our approach to the source of this help.

Your own higher self is the best means of introduction to your spirit teacher. Go to your quiet place and contact your higher self by the method we just explained. When you are aware of the presence, say something like, "George, I am ready to seek my first conscious contact with my spirit teacher. Please help me now." Repeat your request, then relax and await the response. Again, it is necessary to be alert and aware of the little things which are slightly out of the ordinary.

Since your spirit teacher is himself (or herself) a complete entity, the method of response may be much more varied than the normally internal response of your "George." It would be quite normal to feel a gentle touch on some part of your body, or a cool breath on your cheek. Or you might see a ball of mist before you, one or more lights of almost any size, or even a full-sized human shape in a soft misty light. You may hear a voice in your ear, or feel a wave of electricity pass through your body, or you may simply be impressed with a new thought of some kind.

When you recognize that first response, answer immediately. Don't choke up with fear! This is a normal and natural occurrence. Answer with a heartfelt, "Thank you," and, "It's wonderful to know you are here." Then ask for the name of your teacher and the recognition symbol he will send to let you know of his presence. As you progress in this work you will undoubtedly attract many teachers. Each will have his own recognition symbol so you can know who is with you at all times.

To you doubters: *This is not a bunch of hogwash!* The spirit world is just as real as the material world, and it is certainly as important to you. Give this a good solid, open-minded try before you dismiss it as nonsense! One good contact is all that is necessary to show you its reality.

How beings from the next dimension can help you

A few words on *why* may make this particular *how* a little easier to understand. Why should beings from the next dimension want to help you? Our answer comes clearly from the concept of one God, one universe, one life, and one consciousness. Dwellers in the spirit world, not blinded by the demands of our physical existence, naturally understand this. They know that we are all *one* in essence, and their individual progress is best furthered by contributing to the overall progress of the species.

Obviously there is only a small portion of our present population which is ready to accept the reality of spirit helpers and to try to work with them. So *you* are extremely important as a potential channel for their work *down here.* This is merely a restatement of the ancient truism, "As you turn to God, God turns to you." We are saying, "As you turn to the spirit world, it turns eagerly to you." One of the best avenues of growth for those on the spirit side of life is active help and participation in the evolution of those souls who are currently struggling for growth within the confines of a material body. Thus we can be sure of the wonderful mutuality of spirit relationships—helping you helps them!

Now specifically *how can they help you?* Any way you can imagine another flesh-and-blood human being helping, and a few ways known only to spirit! Let's look at some real-life examples.

A man was finalizing his divorce, and seriously wondering if there is such a thing as true marital bliss on this earth. He had begun to study and search for spiritual truth, however, and during a period of extreme loneliness he reached a new understanding. He reasoned: "I have just conclusively proved that my judgment in the area of marriage is such that I am totally unqualified to choose a mate for myself. But I am not willing to accept a sentence of loneliness for the rest of my life, so I must seek help from a higher intelligence."

In the quiet of his apartment he reached out for contact with his spirit teacher, and asked for help like this: "Professor, I know that Infinite Spirit knows the whereabouts of the perfect companion for me. I know that, within myself, I have not enough vision to pick her, but *Spirit can*. I ask your help in leading me to her now. Thank you for this gift of divine companionship." He repeated this request each evening at bedtime, talking to his professor just as you would talk to a friend or neighbor who you were sure really wanted to help you.

In less than two weeks he felt a powerful urge to visit a strange church. There a medium told him that a wonderful girl was about to enter his life, and followed with a description which included her hair style and color, the color of her eyes, and her first name. He continued his daily prayer, and two weeks later met the girl who matched the medium's description, but at another church not previously known to himself or the medium. The couple's spiritual affinity was obvious from the very beginning, and each found a depth of feeling and companionship more wonderful than either had dared dream possible. They have been happily married for many years now, and the passage of time has added nothing but richness to their relationship. This was not coincidence or accident! It was the

certain working of spiritual law. Your birthright is fullness of joy
and expression on all planes and in all areas of your life. Now
is the time to claim it!

Another man became interested in working with the spirit world, but it seemed that he could find no time for study or
meditation. In order to hold his job, he was required to attend
meetings in the evening on little notice and with such regular-
ity that it made any kind of spiritual work out of the question.
He came to me for advice and we reasoned together as follows:
In this materially oriented civilization it is absolutely necessary
for a man to work and earn the kind of comfortable living he
feels his family deserves. However, a balanced life must also
include time for recreation, a normal home life, and spiritual
study. Naturally the man agreed, but then came his problem: "I
obviously need to find a different job where I can still make a
good living, but I can't afford to quit and go several weeks
without income, and I certainly don't have time for job hunting
while I'm on my present schedule."

But here was a problem tailor-made for spirit help. He was
really trying to meet all his obligations and still find time for
spiritual work. The only missing factor appeared to be his permission for spirit to help him. He entered his own place of
silence and simply presented his problem to his spirit teachers
with a heartfelt request for help. He repeated this process each
evening just before retiring.

On the afternoon of the fourth day he received a phone
call from an old business acquaintance, asking if he knew of
anyone who might be available for a position with his company. The old associations were fresh and pleasant enough that it
took only two telephone conversations to agree on terms and
salary for the new job. He immediately gave notice, and two
weeks later he began his new career, but this time with ample
opportunity for his spiritual studies. Happily he remembered
his obligation to spirit, and he has progressed wonderfully in
spiritual growth while steadily improving his economic lot.

Let's look at one more quick example before we move
along. A woman was waiting for the traffic signal to change at

a busy intersection. Just as it turned to "go" she reached for the gear shift to move on, but somehow her hand grabbed the ignition key and turned off the motor instead. While she was restarting her motor, a speeding vehicle came from nowhere through the intersection against the light. That evening in her quiet place she received this answer from her spirit teacher: "The only way I could keep you from being hit in that intersection was to make your hand turn off the motor." Yes, many serious mishaps are avoided by the direct intervention of beneficent spirit forces.

Again a word of caution is in order. Just because a person comes to you without a physical body is not total assurance that he (or she) knows any more about the true nature of life than you do. We are given this admonition in the Bible: *Beloved, believe not every spirit, but try the spirits whether they are of God: because many false prophets are gone out into the world.* (1 John 4:1)

John continues by prescribing a test: *Hereby know ye the Spirit of God: Every spirit that confesseth that Jesus Christ is come in the flesh is of God: And every spirit that confesseth not that Jesus Christ is come in the flesh is not of God: and this is that spirit of antichrist, whereof ye have heard that it should come; and even now already is it in the world.* (1 John 4:2, 3)

In modern language, treat any new spirit with the same friendly but cautious reserve you would use on a stranger who knocked on your front door. See that he qualifies himself to you by his words and actions before you place too much trust in him.

Your spirit guides and protectors

It will pay you to spend as much time as possible getting acquainted with your spirit teacher. When you can recognize his presence easily, and your confidence in him is born out of your own happy experience, you are ready to meet other members of your spirit *band*. It is not unusual for one *earth being* to work with a band of from six to twenty-four spirits who devote a great deal of time to the affairs of just this one group. The composition of your group will be unique in character, matching your own special personality. The direction of your natural talents and aptitudes is often obvious from the backgrounds and earthly occupations of the closer members of your band.

If you want to be a musician, for instance, you will undoubtedly find several musicians in your group; but you may also find a doctor, two or three American Indians, an artist and business manager. Each one comes to fulfill a specific function in furthering your spiritual progress and other spiritual works.

Most of us don't regularly recognize every member of our band, but this isn't mandatory. A friend can accomplish many favors for you while you are unaware of his efforts. Again this is that wonderfully mutual situation where helping you helps them, so always give thanks to your teachers for your "lucky breaks"; but don't worry too much about which individual arranged them for you.

As your spiritual unfoldment progresses, you may experience new urges toward achievement along some line of creative endeavor, and this may attract new members into your band. One woman began her serious study of the spirit world and soon felt a vague urge to paint. At about the same time she noticed two new presences during her meditations, and politely asked them how they would identify themselves. Each showed her a symbol of a painting in a golden frame—one was a landscape, the other a portrait. Thus she learned how these two spirits hoped to improve their knowledge and ability to paint by helping her. She spent several days in the library reading about artists and techniques before she finally bought her first artist's supplies. The beautiful work she now turns out is a delight to her family and friends. It carries a shimmering ethereal quality and somehow seems to bring a personal message to each individual who stops to admire it.

Spirit is interested in the unfoldment of *you!* Your spirit friends are capable of helping in any way you will accept. But they will never act as servants in the sense of doing things for you that you should do for yourself. However, they will be zealous in their assistance of your unfoldment in any way that might add beauty or inspiration to life. The more people who stand to benefit from your success, the greater will be spirit's effort on your behalf. In elementary physics we learn of simple machines by which man has been able to amplify his puny strength. The lever, the pulley, and the inclined plane are examples. By these simple devices man gains what is called a *mechanical advantage.* Similarly, by working with the spirit world, man gains a *spiritual advantage* which can manifest as tangible help in any worthwhile undertaking.

Enjoy your newly found friends. You will find them loyal and helpful. But remember that working with spirit is like using a physical machine. Spirit will happily amplify the force that you supply, but *you must apply some force.*

How to reach out to the infinite

The purpose of all life seems to be continuous unfoldment or evolution. Through the law of natural selection nature tends constantly to improve each species by the survival and reproduction of the fittest. Man often tampers with this law of selection for his own benefit. By scientific breeding, the poultry of today has been made so much better than that of just fifty years ago that you would no longer buy meat from the older strains. Luther Burbank became world famous for his development of superior plants. Everywhere, man is helping nature do things better. The only major exception seems to be in the improvement of the species of mankind itself.

But what is necessary to the improvement of the species, my fellow beings? Logically it is the same basic kind of cooperation with nature that has improved everything else. However, in man's case we encounter one big difference. As a self-conscious, abstract-thinking entity, one man is quite the same in his evolutionary potential as a whole species of plants or lower animals. You can exercise a process of planned evolution upon yourself and produce results every bit as startling and important as Luther Burbank achieved with his plants. In doing so, you will blaze a new path to achievement for all the souls who follow after.

The path of self-improvement or unfoldment logically leads us into a deeper and more meaningful relationship with the source of all life, the Creator of the Universe. The history of man's seeking this at-one-ment with God reveals two quite different paths: the inner path of love, called mysticism; and the outer path of power, called occultism. Let's examine them briefly as follows.

THE MYSTIC'S APPROACH

Traditionally, the mystic spends a life of quiet contemplation, experiencing God's love in the sunshine and rain, the birds and bees, flowers, trees, and even the thorns. The mystic reasons: Since God is infinite, he is equally present everywhere; so by contemplation of the essence of my own being I must finally experience deity at the center of my being. And through this, I will feel my oneness with all of creation. The keynote of the mystic is *love* of everything as the ultimate form of worship of God.

THE OCCULT APPROACH

The occult approach is one of action. The occultist reasons: The great unseen forces which created the universe must still be operating or it would collapse back into the nothingness from where it came. So by learning to direct these forces I can influence the course of creation and thus become more nearly one with God by performing more of His creative functions. The keynote of the occultist is *achievement* as the ultimate demonstration of worship of God.

THE BALANCED, COMBINED APPROACH

The great pitfall of mysticism is the development of a beautifully loving impracticality of existence, while the danger facing the occultist is the tendency to become a coldly calculating egomaniac. Either one is way out of balance! But the solution to this problem is obvious. Why not follow a combined approach, balancing the coldly practical occultism with the warmth of deep mystical experience? This will be the theme of all our study of practical applications of E.S.P. and spirit contact. The truly spiritual approach to the infinite is loving application of the self to improving all areas of the particular. The richer and fuller your life, the more you are fulfilling your destiny as a thinking being.

How to gain complete personal protection

We have looked at several examples of spirit help that amount to protection of your physical being. Now let's discuss ways and means of insuring this help for you, not only for your physical being, but also for all your physical, mental, emotional, and spiritual affairs.

Our example from the science of physics is again in point. Spirit generally works by amplifying your own efforts, so we must look first at what you can do to help yourself.

In discussing what they call accident-prone people, modern psychologists recognize the fact that most accidents are *attracted*. It is a short step from there to the realization that accidents never just happen, they are caused by people; and the happy occurrences which save others from harm are also caused by people. Your studies are making you more and more aware of the unseen forces whose existence provides your means of extrasensory experience. Even our scientifically oriented society is accustomed to similar unseen things—at least one airliner crash was attributed to interference with the craft's communication system by a tiny transistor radio being operated in the passenger cabin.

We can logically infer that there is some quality of human consciousness which attracts trouble and accidents, and some other quality which tends to repel them. Some people manifest a certain intensity of consciousness that overshadows even their physical senses to a degree, and may make others within their proximity downright uncomfortable. This is the consciousness of the accident-prone, the jinx that attracts disaster of all shapes and sizes. We all produce some degree of this negative consciousness when we become tense or overanxious, and simply learning to eliminate these conditions will be a major step forward. The greater your success in achieving the *relaxed awareness* we discussed in Chapter 1, the more you will be eliminating the sources of trouble. The achievement of a reasonable degree of relaxed awareness is a prerequisite for obtaining effective protection through the aid of our friends in the spirit world.

Let's contemplate the nature of the next dimension as a means of understanding the mechanics of spirit protection. Without the impediment of the sluggish reactions of dense matter, dwellers in the spirit realm must find the mind to be a somewhat different tool than it is on our lower earth plane. Here *below,* thought is certainly creative, but it is impeded by the inertia of material objects. But mental creation and even travel in the spirit realm are essentially instantaneous. This also gives a completely different meaning to the concept of time. Thus to a tremendous extent, each spirit lives in a world of his own mental creation; and this is formed at first from the beliefs and quality of consciousness he brought with him from his earth life. Then it is modified by his newly acquired knowledge and experience as his spirit life progresses.

Thus a criminal or ne'er-do-well passing into spirit will probably enter a world of misery and hate, such as we might expect his mind to create. Now if such an entity should wander into your quiet place and try to communicate with you, you would be in danger of being deceived or even driven toward some negative act. The Bible often speaks of *spirit possession* as an affliction like any other disease. Modern science pooh-poohs this as ancient superstition, but there are those in mental hospitals today who might return to normal lives with a little old-fashioned "casting out of 'evil' spirits." Since such entities will enter only a thought atmosphere which is compatible with their own, you can best avoid them by maintaining an attitude of happy spiritual aspiration. Fill your quiet place with your own bright spiritual light, then you can expect the most help from your spirit band.

Let's return to the Bible for help in this understanding. Creation is associated with light: *And God said, Let there be light and there was light. And God saw the light, that it was good: and God divided the light from the darkness.* (Genesis 1:3, 4) In the world of spirit, those who have gained understanding live in the light, while the confused souls dwell in a darkness of their own creation. Now if you have been in a dark room for some time, and someone suddenly turns on a bright light, you experience a very real discomfort. In much the same way, those spirits who dwell in the darkness cannot stand a bright spiritual light. Thus your effective prayer for protection is: "I dwell in the bright Christ Light, all goodness is attracted to me, and nothing of the darkness can come near me; I give thanks for the wonderful light."

Use this prayer each time you enter your quiet place for meditation, and *any time* you feel uncomfortable. Spirit protection is yours for the asking. It can be the most positive influence in your life. Use the little prayer just on general principles at least five times every day: "I dwell in the bright Christ Light, all goodness is attracted to me, and nothing of the darkness can come near me; I give thanks for the wonderful light."

Your special place in the divine scheme of things

Wherever we look in this tremendous universe, we see order and organization. From the tiny particles which make up one atom to the vast galaxies of space, man has observed a consistent manifestation of law and intelligence which keeps the electrons in their orbits around the atomic nuclei and the planets in their paths around the suns. If this were not so, the universe would disintegrate into a giant chaotic mess. Behind all manifestation is an Intelligence minute enough to control individual electrons, yet vast enough to direct the course of whole galaxies. There can be no doubt that this Infinite Intelligence has some sort of a master plan for the development of its manifestations.

From our vantage point astride this speck of dust we call the Earth, we are in position to understand only a tiny fraction of the Creator's overall plan. But how much is a fraction of infinity? The part *we can experience now* is close enough to infinite that we won't know the difference for many incarnations to come. Now how should we perceive mankind's part in the Divine Plan? How can you discover your special part in it?

Life, as we are able to observe it, is embarked on an apparently endless spiral of evolution or improvement. So far, man is the only earthly manifestation of self-consciousness with the power of choice best described as initiative and selection. Therefore we are the first earth beings with the power to choose whether or not we will cooperate with the laws of evolution. To continue to ignore the laws leaves us no worse off than we have ever been, but what is the potential reward of complete cooperation? Isn't it the achievement of a new level of consciousness where man understands the true meaning of being created in the image and likeness of God?

In truth, we are intended to grow into the realization that man is God in potential, here and now! And we should begin to demonstrate this truth by manifesting beauty, peace, abundance, love, and joy as a beacon of hope for all those who have not yet grown to this beautiful realization. Now why are you so important to this Divine Plan? Precisely because this great realization must be experienced by *individuals!* Since the realization and the *power* both exist only deep within the recesses of individual beings, you as an individual are the only avenue through which mankind can achieve this great evolutionary advance. Thus, as you help yourself the most, you simultaneously make your most important contribution to the advancement of mankind.

You are entitled to tangible help from spirit in every phase of your existence. But isn't it logical that spirit will tend to shower the greatest help on those who are consciously striving for the advancement of the common cause by the sincere improvement of their own beings? The Master left us this same thought when He said: *And seek ye not what ye shall eat, or what ye shall drink, neither be ye of doubtful mind. For all these things do the nations of the world seek after: and your Father knoweth that ye have need of these things. But rather seek ye the kingdom of God; and all these things shall be added unto you.*

Spiritual growth is the key to all progress, happiness, fulfillment, and joy. Join your spirit teachers in mutual seeking, and you will unfold a life of joy beyond the limits of imagination.

POINTS TO REMEMBER

I. All major religions have a heritage of spirit contact.

II. Purify your "temple" before seeking contact.

III. Start by contacting your higher self.

IV. Ask your higher self to introduce you to your spirit teachers.

V. Ask for help whenever you need it.

VI. Live always in the bright light of spirit protection.

VII. Find your place in the Divine Plan and grow in joy, usefulness, and fulfillment.

how to
Attain Perfect Health
for Yourself and Others

Let's begin our quest for perfect health by agreeing that any healing is good, regardless of the method by which it is attained. Some religious and occult sects preach against doctors and medicines, but this is obviously foolishness. Divine protection is a fact for many of the faithful, but if you have a physical problem, it simply shows that you haven't yet attained the perfect consciousness of protection. So why suffer needlessly when medicine can help?

The value of modern medicine

The science of medicine has unquestionably grown up into sophisticated adulthood. Through applied research it has extended our average life expectancy in the last fifty years, and made the process of daily living more comfortable along the way. As the frontiers of medicine push ever forward, dread killer diseases of years ago are one by one becoming only bad memories. To deny the good works of medicine would be ridiculous, but to consider it the only hope or the omnipotent fighter of disease would be equally silly. Let's quickly agree that there is a time when any prudent individual should consult a competent medical doctor.

Certainly you would expect to let a good doctor set your broken leg or stitch up a nasty cut. And for any persistent ache or pain, it is a good idea to let your physician decide whether there is an organic problem. Then pay attention to the diagnosis and submit to expert treatment. But we should carefully understand that doctors treat the symptoms, or at best the secondary causes of our symptoms. The physician's field is basically restricted to treatment of your physical body; but we will clearly see that all disease originates in the mental or astral bodies. Your doctor does his best with the knowledge and tools at his command, but without your help in removing the mental and emotional causes underlying the symptoms, his results are bound to be limited both in scope and duration.

Don't be misled by this line of reasoning. Some people refuse to take aspirin for a headache because it "doesn't cure the cause." But others take aspirin and find that they are much more comfortable while waiting for nature to remove the cause. And it seems to take the same length of time to remove the cause with or without the medication. There is no reason for you to be foolish about it. *Use anything that will help!*

Then if you should happen to be one of the many people who suffer a physical problem that medicine has not yet cured (or perhaps even found a name for), you can join that growing group of sincere spiritual workers for the comfort and upliftment of man. We call them *spiritual healers.* Most of us who become interested in spiritual healing do so because of personal experience in an area of modern medicine which has not progressed far enough to cure our problem. Then when spiritual healing works for us, we somehow feel bound to repay our spirit friends by helping others. As is so often true in this work, you will find that the best way to help yourself is to set out to learn how to help others. So let's start helping ourselves now by learning the rudiments of spiritual healing.

How you can become a spiritual healer

The big advantage of the spiritual healer is his approach to the individual as a spiritual entity—a whole being, consisting of a soul which is manifesting through mental, emotional, and physical bodies. A simple recognition of the vital energy flow from the emotional body to the physical, as directed by the mental body (or mind), gives the healer more ammunition than all the scalpels and antibiotics in the country. You will learn that every physical symptom is the result of a maladjustment in the energy flow coming into the physical body. Careful cooperation between the patient, the healer, and the spirit forces can always correct the maladjustment and bring about the return to the original health state of the divine archetype.

With only a little practice, you can learn to see the energy field around yourself or your patient so you will know that we are not carrying on a modern witch hunt. The field of energy which holds your physical body in shape and vitalizes it is known as the *aura*. It is most easily noticed around the head or the fingers; but it actually permeates your physical body, and extends beyond it in all directions for several inches in the easily visible light spectra and for much greater distances in the finer, less-visible vibrations. Your first glimpse of your own aura is important because it proves that your body is much more than a mere pile of clay. It is a new look at the *livingness* which is you!

The aura is light. Now if you want to get a careful look at any subtle light source, how do you go about it? Naturally you try to set up conditions that provide a minimum of interference from other light sources or variegated backgrounds. For your first attempt to see your aura, try this simple experiment:

Sit in a room that is dark except for one or two candles burning on the table. Spread a few pieces of clean white paper on the table and against the wall to provide as unbroken a white background as possible. Now hold your hands at a comfortable reading distance in front of you with the palms facing each other and the fingers comfortably curved. Bring your hands near each other until the fingers almost touch, then slowly pull them apart for a distance of 3 to 5 inches. Stare carefully at the space between the tips of your fingers as you move your hands slowly together and then apart. Soon you will notice the shafts of light running between your fingers. You may sense the vibrations more like the *waves of heat* that we often see rising from a dark surface on a hot day. But whether you see light or vibration, watch it stretch thin as you move your fingers apart, then grow fatter as the fingers come closer together again.

Continue the exercise and notice how you are using your eyes when the aura of your fingers seems most visible. Then try to see the aura around your head in a mirror, using your eyes the same way. Next, observe the effect on the aura around your head when you bring your open hand near it Then try a mental exercise: See if you can expand the visible aura around your head by *willing* it. Can you vary its shape? How about changing its color?

Since the aura is a special kind of light, we can learn to turn it into a *healing light*. This, too, is a matter of *will*. You have mentally affected the aura around your head, and the same principle applies to any body part we choose to work with. Start controlling the energy around your hands and directing it to become a most beneficial healing agency for anyone you touch with this light-energy. A good exercise for developing your healing faculty is to sit before a mirror and hold up your hands like a saint giving the benediction; then ask your spirit teachers to join you in sending forth the healing energy to bless all mankind. Feel your hands tingle as the healing energy flows out of them. Regular practice of this universal healing exercise will improve your effectiveness and prepare you for the time when you need to help someone close to you (or even yourself) by using your wonderful new healing hands.

You will have an unquestionably positive effect on *all who cooperate*. An excellent example of the need for the patient's cooperation came in my relationship with a lady in the business world. Because we work fairly close together, I learned that she often suffered from headaches. One day I offered to help her get rid of a bad one she obviously suffered from at the moment. Without telling her what I was doing, I worked with the spirit forces to manipulate the healing energies and easily removed the psychic block which was causing the trouble. In less than five minutes her headache was completely gone and she was very thankful for the assistance. However, she was a rather high-strung individual and managed to produce a new block for herself every few days. For several weeks I was able to cure each headache with dispatch. But finally her curiosity got the better of her and she pointedly asked me how I did this. She had a strong antireligious prejudice, and my explanation unfortunately angered her. From that day forward, I was completely unable to relieve her pain. Her elimination of the element of receptivity blocked the flow of beneficial energy from my hands and even from my spirit helpers, so she resumed her use of aspirin and other medication.

The example serves to illustrate two important points. First, receptivity, or at least the absence of conscious resistance, is definitely required. But second, and perhaps more important, the energy flow itself works primarily on the symptoms. So without the removal of the mental cause, it is no more able to effect a permanent cure than the aspirin. The only way to produce a permanent cure is to move from the mind through the emotions to the physical. Let's begin to examine the following basic steps in spiritual healing.

The five steps to spiritual healing

We will examine the five steps to spiritual healing in detail, but first here they are in brief:

1. Determine the broad mental cause and explain it to the patient.
2. Invoke spirit-world help in breaking the basic thought-reaction patterns of the cause, and in healing the mental, emotional, and physical bodies.

3. With the cooperation of spirit, apply the healing light to the afflicted area (laying on of the hands).

4. Assist the patient in establishing healthy new mental and emotional patterns to prevent further outbreaks. (He must change his way of reacting.)

5. Keep up the prayer and healing work until the patient has completely recovered.

How to determine the mental cause of illness or disease

Obviously no one can make a simple table that says exactly what thought pattern causes each physical disorder. Life isn't nearly that simple. Apparently identical thought patterns in two different individuals may cause a heart attack in one and nothing worse than a simple headache in the other. However, there is some general correlation between the major negative thought patterns and broad groups of physical troubles. In *The Miraculous Laws of Universal Dynamics,* I presented a table of mental poisons and their general symptoms. It seems useful to produce it here with only minor variations from the original.

The table should be studied like a mystical poem, for the *feeling* it produces within you, not for specific case information.

Obviously everyone living here on this earth still has a few negative thought patterns. It will pay you well to look within yourself and root out as many as possible before they have a chance to cause more trouble. For every negative pattern of your own that you notice, you will find that you have a neat bit of mental gymnastics by which you justify harboring such a dangerous felon. It will be an excellent exercise for you to write down each justification, then study it carefully to detect the basic flaw in your reasoning. *Now throw out the negative pattern,* but keep your understanding of the flaw in your rationalization to use in helping someone else get rid of the same sort of mental poison.

Whether the patient is yourself, a loved one, or a complete stranger, his cooperation and straightforward honesty are the keys to success in this part of the treatment. With enthusiastic spirit cooperation you may accomplish a perfect physical healing, but unless you also break up the mental cause, you will discover that the healing is short-lived. This is what Jesus meant when He so often cautioned someone He had just healed, *Go, and sin no more.* The only sins in the universe are negative thought patterns and their manifestations.

TABLE OF MENTAL POISONS AND THEIR SYMPTOMS

Mental Poison	*Resulting Symptoms*
1. Resentment, bitterness, hatred.	Skin rash, boils, blood disorders, allergies, heart trouble, stiff joints.
2. Confusion, frustration, anger.	Common colds; pneumonia; tuberculosis; disorders of the respiratory tract, eyes, nose and throat; asthma.
3. Anxiety, impatience, greed.	High blood pressure, migraine headaches, ulcers, nearsightedness, hard of hearing, heart attacks.
4. Cynicism, pessimism, defeatism.	Low blood pressure, anemia, polio, diabetes, leprosy, low income, kidney disorders.
5. Revulsion, fear, guilt.	Accidents, cancer, personal failure, poverty, poor sex, "bad blood."
6. Antagonism, inferiority, introversion.	Allergies, headaches, lack of friends, heart murmur, accidents.

So how do you discover your patient's mental cause? If it is yourself, by detached introspection; if someone else, by psychic communication and the art of conversation. Caution your patient of the need for directness and honesty, then ask a few simple questions like: "What do you resent the most?" or, "Tell me briefly, what are you most ashamed of?" or, "If a good fairy gave you a choice of one person or condition to be removed from your life, what would you pick?" As you learn to relax during such sessions, you will find that you receive psychic impressions which will also help in your understanding of the problem.

Now let's become fully aware of a most important point. *You are not to be a judge!* The Master cautioned us, *Judge not, lest ye be judged.* Then He demonstrated His practice of what He preached. For instance, there was His conversation with the woman taken in adultery. After they had been left alone, He asked her, *Woman, where are those thine accusers? Hath no man condemned thee?*

She said, *No man, Lord.*

And Jesus said unto her, *Neither do I condemn thee: go and sin no more.* (John 8:10, 11)

No matter how terrible a confession may seem, if you show the slightest revulsion or condemnation, you will lose any ability to help your patient. Discuss all problems with warmth and understanding, and be ever alert to hear the voice within which prompts us to say just the right thing to help your patient reach a new insight. This new understanding is a major factor in the success, since the spirit world is bound to respect an individual's wishes. In other words, it is only when your patient *wants to change* his thought patterns and *asks* for help, that a permanent cure becomes possible.

How the spirit world helps break old reaction patterns

O.K., now your patient wants to change and wants spirit help to accomplish it. Logically it's time to assist him in asking for it.

First call on your own spirit teachers and ask them to invite your patient's teachers to join in prayer. Then, pray aloud somewhat as follows: "Infinite Spirit, in its own way and through the agency of our wonderful helpers from the spirit world, is helping (your patient) to break up all his negative mental and emotional patterns now. His mind is becoming highly sensitized to notice his negative tendencies before they get a chance to manifest as emotions, thus he can choose to react with divine light and love to all situations. He is inspired to find the hidden good in all his experiences and always to let spirit express through him as harmony, health, wealth, peace, unfoldment, and fulfillment. Thus he turns to God, and God answers with showers of blessings. We sit in the now, giving thanks for these wonderful changes."

After a reasonable pause, repeat your prayer, then pause again. Continue until you or your patient feels some form of definite response from spirit. Spirit will always respond by sending positive thought vibrations to the mental body and soothing energy to the emotional body. Your patient may feel a wave of warmth pass through his physical body, or he may describe it as a tingling feeling like a mild electric shock. Others will simply feel a sensation of peace stealing through their being. If you have done your work properly, *there will be a response from spirit!*

You must expect your patient to feel this response. Your faith will help open the path for the downpouring of the beneficent energies. Now you are ready to add your own light to the helpful spirit energies.

How to apply the healing light to the afflicted area

We opened this discussion with exercises to develop your aura vision and your ability to control and direct this visible part of the vital life force. With the help of your spirit teachers, you can direct this powerful force to cleanse and heal the patient's physical body by application through his aura. Understand that the aura is *light* which is in the nature of pure emotional energy, and it can be directed by the mind to produce important tangible effects on the physical body.

The process is simple. Ask your teachers to participate, then mentally direct the powerful light to flow from your aura into the afflicted area of the patient and exert a cleansing, healing influence on both the emotional and physical bodies. As you work in this way, you will make an interesting discovery: You don't lose any vitality in your part of the process. If anything, you will feel invigorated by "giving a healing." This is because you are only acting as a pumping station for the vital energy that is present throughout the atmosphere, and many of your own needs will be met by the rush of vital energy through your system to that of your patient. How should we go about this?

If your patient is present, the best method of applying the healing energies is by the laying on of the hands. Prepare your patient by sitting him in a straight chair with the back turned around to one side, leaving you clear access to his spine and the seven major psychic centers (see Chapter 1). Prepare yourself by holding out your hands, palms up, and taking a deep breath. While holding the breath, mentally send a short prayer to your spirit teachers to help in directing the healing energies through you to the patient. Then hold your palm about 4 inches apart and feel the energy flowing between them. You can tell the energy is flowing by the tingling sensations that one hand seems to be sending, while the other receives the energy your body is pumping between them, much like an electric current.

Begin your treatment by placing your *sending hand* on or near the base of the patient's spine. Now hold your *receiving hand* about an inch above your patient's head, and move it around until you feel the maximum current flowing up into your outstretched palm. At different times this flow of energy may feel hot or cold or just tingly, but you should always feel something, no matter how slight. Hold this position and let the current flow for about 60 seconds. Then keep your receiving hand in place, but move your sending hand up to the area of the spleen center. Again hold this position and let the current flow for about a minute. Next, go on with your sending hand to the point on the spine directly behind the solar plexus and let the energy flow some more. Repeat the process for each of the first six psychic centers. When you are ready to treat the seventh or crown center, move your receiving hand to the forehead directly above the eyes, and this time feel the flow from the crown center out through the brow center. As you get used to working with the energies, you will develop your own techniques and variations because some things will feel more natural and effective for you than others. This is good, since no two really effective healers ever seem to use identical techniques. Even the same individual healer will find his techniques evolving with time, and also adjusting themselves to meet the needs of particular patients.

Now that you have cleared the seven major centers with your healing light, you are ready to concentrate on the specific area of your patient's symptoms. As best you can in the particular circumstances, get the afflicted area between the palms of your hands and will the energy to flow again. It helps to mentally picture a rushing stream of light flowing from your sending hand through the afflicted area and back into the receiving hand. Picture this light as the spiritual equivalent of a swirling torrent of water which sweeps everything of a diseased or negative nature before it back into the nothingness from where it came.

End the treatment with a prayer of thanks to your spirit teachers and the Heavenly Father for the perfect healing of your patient. Visualize him as absolutely whole, complete, pure, and perfect, expressing more and more of the God-life as he continually grows in spiritual understanding. Then release him to God and *go wash your hands,* while mentally affirming that you are washing away any remaining trace of negativity. If you forget this ceremonial cleansing process of the hand washing, you may pick up a few of your patient's symptoms and wind up needing a healing for yourself.

Don't get the idea that this is just for professional healers!

You can use it to help your spouse or child, or even your pet. And it will benefit your own spiritual growth for the trying. By willingly giving of yourself to help someone else, you make it easier for your teachers to send help to you. Don't scoff at this or shrug it off! Develop your healing ability now, so you will be ready to help someone who really needs it tomorrow or the day after.

If you know of someone who needs healing help, but you can't be present, you can still participate. Go to your quiet place and call on your teachers to help. Then mentally picture the whole process being administered to the patient by your spirit healing teachers. Again end the *treatment* with a prayer of thanks and a visualization of your patient as absolutely whole and perfect. And again *wash your hands* for your own protection and to gain a feeling of release. This is called *absent treatment*. You will be amazed at the excellent results you get with just a little practice.

How to establish healthy mental and emotional reaction patterns

Now the healing is well under way, and our main concern is to prevent recurrence of the mental causes. A simple explanation of the interrelatedness of the whole of the human entity will be most beneficial. Logically show your patient that he is a soul expressing through mental, emotional, and physical vehicles; and he must look upon the self as a whole being rather than a group of isolated parts. Use the example of psychosomatic medicine to demonstrate that the mind and emotions have a definite effect on the physical body. Then follow with the next step—a healthy mental and emotional pattern must have a positive, healing effect on the physical body.

Convince your patient that he can't afford to harbor negativity. Then review the trouble areas you turned up while seeking the mental cause of his problem. Help him find new and positive attitudes to replace the newly uprooted negative ones. Review and repeat the teaching until you are convinced you are really getting through to him. The ultimate success of the entire treatment depends on the effectiveness of the joint effort to change the underlying thought patterns. Your own completely positive approach to life is the best possible argument. It will show through your words and win for you if you have taken the trouble to develop it. Similarly, any negativity that you demonstrate will work to the detriment of the healing process, and could even make the patient worse. Work constantly to improve your personal attitudes and reactions to help yourself and your ability to inspire others.

Keep working until the healing is complete

Some healings are dramatic and instantaneous, but these are relatively rare, and they often degenerate into a relapse later. By far the most common and the surest healings are the result of a form of growth. Now the most obvious quality of physical growth is its lack of noticeable speed. A seed sprouts and sends the first little shoot up through the ground, then the tiny plant slowly unfolds, and even more slowly grows into a bush or tree. The naked eye is not capable of registering the moment-to-moment progress of the growth of a plant or a human baby, but we know that it is growing all the same. Careful observation from week to week or month to month reveals definite progress.

Such is the normal progress of spiritual healing. New life and muscle is added to a shriveled limb or a useless eye, one cell at a time, and this only by faith and constant vigilance to prevent the negativity of the cause from returning. Certainly there are instantaneous healings like those recorded in the Bible as accomplishments of the Master, but if your initial attempts are not so spectacular, there is still no reason to give up. In the world of track, the distance runner will tell you it's not so much the start, but the finish, of the race that counts. Many a mile run has been won by a person who was fifty yards behind the leader at the half-mile point. Success comes to the person who doesn't quit! A man who keeps trying in the face of failure is called dumb and stubborn until he succeeds, then he is lauded for his insight and perseverance. You can't win a fight unless you get up one more time than you are knocked down!

Keep your faith! Work until the healing is complete and can be verified by medical doctors or anyone else who may care to pay attention.

Some seeds take longer than others to put a sprout above the ground. One sure way to prevent results is to keep digging up your seeds to see if they have started to sprout. The Master had an excellent bit of advice for this situation: *If ye have faith as a grain of mustard seed, ye shall say unto this mountain, Remove hence to yonder place; and it shall remove; and nothing shall be impossible to you.* (Matt. 17.20)

How to heal yourself

Basically the same five steps apply to any healing, whether it is given to yourself or to someone else; but it will be worthwhile to review the process as it is applied to your own body and affairs.

1. Determine the mental cause. This step always seems easier for someone else, just as it is easy to look over someone's shoulder and tell him what he is doing wrong. If your most objective searching fails to turn up the mental cause, ask your spirit teachers for help. Then pay careful attention; you will be tempted to shrug off the answer as not applying to you, but no matter how absurd it may seem at first, face up to it. In some stubborn cases you may consider seeking help from another student of the healing art. In any case, root out the trouble no matter how much effort it takes!

2. Seek spirit-world help in breaking the old negative reaction patterns. Your spirit teachers are anxious to answer your calls for help. Now that you have determined the mental cause, it is well to renew your request for help in breaking the negative thought patterns each morning just as you get out of bed. Again, pay attention! The more you cooperate and listen for the promptings of spirit, the quicker will you get rid of the mental poisons.

3. With the help of spirit, apply the healing light to the afflicted area. For yourself it is just like giving someone else an *absent healing.* Sit quietly and visualize your spirit healer applying the light by laying on his own hands. Then feel the light as it surges through each of your major psychic centers and moves on to cleanse and renew the problem area.

4. Establish healthy mental and emotional patterns to prevent new outbreaks. This step is much more important for you than for any of your patients because you are working to activate your psychic faculties and thus are more sensitive to all your thoughts and reactions. The best possible advice on this subject was given by the apostle Paul: *Finally, brethren, whatsoever things are true, whatsoever things are honest, whatsoever things are just, whatsoever things are pure, whatsoever things are lovely, whatsoever things are of good report; if there be any virtue, and if there be any praise, think on these things.* (Phil. 4:8)

5. Keep working until the healing is perfect. Since we are so very susceptible to our own thoughts, it is of greater importance than ever that we do not become discouraged. According to your faith is it done unto you.

Learn to live constantly in the healing light. To the extent that you are successful in mentally living in the pure white light you will be healed of all your present problems, and you will remain radiantly healthy and happy until you are ready to lay down this physical shell and graduate to the next in the spirit world.

Expect excellent results

The level of confidence that you project to your patient is a key factor in the success of the treatment. However, it is not your outward expressions so much as your inner feelings that control your projected faith. The healer must remain completely optimistic throughout the course of the treatment, giving thanks to spirit for each tiny physical manifestation of improvement. And when no outward manifestation is yet visible, you should continue giving thanks for the fact that the healing forces are acting so effectively on the unseen side of life that the healing is about to show through into the physical, like a bud suddenly opening into a beautiful blossom.

A man suffered terribly from a spine infection called Pott's disease, for which the medical profession had not yet found a cure. His seeking of some form of help led him to a small Spiritualist Church where the twice-a-week services began with individual spiritual healing treatments for all who would accept them. He instinctively felt a great power there, and began attending each service with a prayer for help in his heart. The philosophy imparted by the sermons slowly helped change many previously negative thought patterns, while the healing light administered through the laying on of the healer's hands continually cleansed his physical body. It is difficult to imagine such a slow, and yet so steady, improvement in a condition. After the third week his regular answer to the question, "How are you feeling?" was, "Better." And he did get better, mentally, financially, emotionally, and physically. At the end of the first year his doctors were amazed that his spine had completely ceased draining, and the deformity was noticeably reduced. No one would care to say exactly when the healing was complete. He still takes his twice-a-week treatments for the benefits of well-being in other areas of his life as well as for the peace of mind that comes from knowing that the old problems can never come back through that wonderful light.

Not all good healings take that long. A business executive developed a huge hemorrhoid. He decided to postpone the recommended surgery for two weeks because of pressing business. During this period he sought spiritual help. A simple pattern of anxiety coupled with lack of physical exercise was noted by the healer. An intensive program of twice daily absent treatments by the healer, coupled with a simple yoga exercise, relieved all the pain in two days. Within a week there was no evidence of a hemorrhoid at all. Thus he avoided both the time loss from work and a very painful operation.

A migraine sufferer was accustomed to being knocked out by her attacks to the point of simply going to bed until they passed. Generally she had an attack about every ten days which lasted twelve to thirty-six hours. One evening she arrived at a spiritual gathering to take part in a ways-and-means discussion, but an attack had begun to hit her while driving to the meeting. She sank into a chair and commented that she would have to head for home and bed, and she "sure hoped she could make it that far." The work was new to this sufferer, so she was amazed when two women suggested she stretch out on the couch and let them try to help her. They formed a human-spirit chain, with one woman sending the powerful light into the patient's head while the other pulled it out through her feet, and the spirit helpers purified it and completed the circuit back to the first healer. Within ten minutes all the pain was removed, and the patient was able to enjoy the meeting and go home afterwards with a living hope for a new pain-free life. No, this was not her last migraine headache, but the attacks were quickly reduced in frequency to about three a year of a much milder variety. After three years of study and practice, she was able to report no headaches that couldn't be relieved by simply taking a couple of aspirin tablets.

It is not necessary to accept any physical condition as incurable. The same forces which built your body are available to repair it. The price of the repair job is complete cooperation with the great healing forces of the spirit world!

How to handle special healing problems

Sometimes a physical problem is aggravated by seemingly impossible surroundings such as extreme poverty, a totally sadistic spouse or head of the family, unrequited love, or a career that is obviously slipping due to the force of circumstances. An individual may have been born into a difficult situation in order to learn some special lesson, and no healing can be expected to be successful until the lesson is digested. At times like these you should give extra thanks that it is not you who performs the healing. The power of God manifesting through your spirit helpers performs the healings, and it is as infinite as you are willing to believe.

Any time you feel that external conditions are a major stumbling block to the healing efforts, talk it over with your spirit teachers and ask for their help. Often a joint meditation with your patient will quickly reveal the basic lesson required, or some simple change of approach to the patient's thinking habits which will be the key to a perfect healing. Of course, you are working with a whole being which you cannot isolate from its surroundings, but regardless of any astrological or karmic influences, each individual is entitled to grow constantly into better and better conditions of health, finances, happiness, peace, and joy. Teach your patient that this is his birthright, and encourage him to claim it every moment of his life.

Mental cases present a different problem of approach. Obviously it will accomplish little to reason with a catatonic or a paranoid who is playing Napoleon. In these cases the laying on of hands can often work wonders, but we must take care not to frighten or unduly excite the patient. The soundest and surest approach is directly from the spirit side of life. If the trouble is being caused by obsessing entities, spirit-world intervention may be the only way to reach your patient. Group healing prayer and requests for help from the assembled spirit teachers of the group can produce enough force to bring any patient back to some greater degree of rationality. Seek whatever help you feel is appropriate. Certainly this is a most wholesome time to prove the promise of the Master: *Ask, and it shall be given you; seek, and ye shall find; knock, and it shall be opened unto you.* (Luke 11:9-13)

Use your healing ability as often as possible

Whether you use it to help yourself, your family, or all mankind, you must agree that proficiency in the healing art is a gift of great value. But like the mind or a muscle, it requires the right exercise to develop its maximum utility. A muscle will atrophy with disuse, or a mind will become dim; and so it is with your ability to assist the spirit world with the healing process. Never hesitate to help! If your assistance would be misinterpreted or resented, give it silently at the altar of your own heart, and tell no one. When you can help by injecting yourself directly into the situation with prayer and laying on of hands, all the better.

In truth we are all one, and anything you do to help someone else *must help you* as well. The Master expressed this thought: *And the King shall answer and say unto them, Verily I say unto you, Inasmuch as ye have done it unto one of the least of these my brethren, ye have done it unto me.* (Matt. 25:40)

You don't have to get yourself a reputation as "that nut who is always butting in trying to heal somebody," but with discretion, tact, and prayer you can perform many healing miracles for the good of your brethren. As you give of yourself in loving service, you are blessed in many more ways than you can imagine. Add this as a new dimension to your life, now!

POINTS TO REMEMBER

I. Modern medicine is good. Never hesitate to call on it.

II. The spiritual healer treats his patient's whole being by redirecting the energy flow from the astral or emotional to the physical body.

III. Learn to see your aura, and mentally vary its size and shape.

IV. Practice directing the flow of healing energy from your hands.

 V. The five steps of spiritual healing are:

    A. Determine the mental cause.

    B. Seek spirit help both in breaking the negative thought-reaction patterns and in the physical healing.

    C. Apply the healing light to the afflicted area.

    D. Help establish new healthy mental and emotional patterns.

    E. Keep working until the healing is complete.

VI. In working with negative mental patterns, judge not! Merely heal.

VII. Expect excellent healing results.

VII. Practice often.

how to
Use E.S.P. to Gain Riches in Ever-Increasing Abundance

Ever since society became complex enough to outgrow the barter system, people have suffered from real and fancied troubles with money. The average American feels that he is restricted in his ability to express himself and accomplish worthwhile things by his lack of unlimited funds. A special few inherit great material wealth, then have to strive all the harder to keep it from destroying their ambition and drive. Since money is some kind of problem to almost everybody, a closer look at what it really is will help us get better control of our relationship to it.

A new look at riches

What is money, anyway? For most of us it has long since ceased to be pieces of silver or green ink on pieces of paper. Now, money is simply a few assorted numbers appearing as an abstract thing we call our bank balance. We all tend to become greatly excited over nothing where our bank accounts are concerned. You will say, "Not me!" But let's think about it. The mathematical symbol for nothing is zero, which we express as *0*. If your next bank statement arrived with one or two symbols of nothing placed between the numbers and the decimal point, *you would get excited!* But if it showed a check charged against you with the same extra nothings inserted, *you would panic.*

Money is simply a symbol, an *idea,* a convenient way of measuring your claim to future goods and services. We entered this classroom called Earth to learn to be masters of life. Our purpose is to control and direct our ideas, *not to be enslaved by them.* We are intended to express more and more of life, not limitation. The Master taught us simply on this matter: *And ye shall know the truth, and the truth shall make you free.* (John 8:32)

I am come that they might have life, and that they might have it more abundantly. (John 10:10)

The Gospels are full of examples of Jesus using the higher laws for what we might call economic purposes. He turned water into wine, found His tax money in a fish's mouth, and more than once fed the multitudes by dramatically multiplying a food supply. Clearly the great Christian example taught us not to accept material limitations. We must learn to recognize apparent shortages of money as glorious opportunities to develop our mastery over Earth life.

Begin to become a magnet now; attune your being to riches. A young man had an idea for a product which he was sure would make life more enjoyable for many people. He had only $100 to spend toward promoting it. Most of us would despair and submit to the limitation, thinking "This is just too big for me to attempt." This man managed to produce a few samples from materials he wheedled from his potential suppliers. So he spent his $100 for the biggest advertisement it would buy. He sold enough from the first go-round that he had $300 to spend on advertising the next week. Instead of just spending the $300 on advertising, he borrowed another $300 from a friend and spent the whole works on advertising. His confidence prompted him to continue pyramiding his business spending, and in less than three years he sold his company for several million dollars.

The reason this doesn't happen every day is the lack of confidence in an idea that makes a man give the *extra bit of himself,* which is the ingredient of all success. You are standing on the threshold of greater financial success than you have dared to dream. Let's step across!

How to interest your spirit helpers in bringing you riches

Many religionists have a terrible habit of degrading money, both in their thinking and from the pulpit. It is a crime against the well-being of humanity to preach that money is filthy lucre or that love of money is the root of all evil. As long as you make the awful mistake of believing these things, your spirit helpers will naturally strive to help you avoid any unpleasant contact with nice-sized sums of money.

It is time to understand the truth. *Love of money is a good emotion!* To love money is to use it wisely and spend it happily in the comfortable knowledge that there is an abundant supply. The negative emotion concerning money is *greed*. But this is exactly the opposite of love, because greed is *fear* of lack. To clutch and hoard money in fear of not having enough is a powerful prayer for poverty. But financial comfort is simply a proper understanding of the laws of earthly living.

You agreed to be born into this particular Earth life to further your personal evolution and thus advance the whole species we call man. Part of coming back into material existence is a set of physical requirements for the proper maintenance of the vehicle of manifestation, and these needs must be met so long as you remain here. You are given your own unique equipment for supplying these needs as you grow toward the age of responsibility. You have a set of aptitudes that fit you for some particular kind of loving service which will allow you to *earn* your keep. And you have a mind which equips you to discover your potentials and develop them. Let's be sure we understand that you don't have to be the economic breadwinner to earn your keep.

A child earns his way in a very real sense by entering wholeheartedly into the growth process. No amount of money can express the feeling of joy in a parent's heart that comes from seeing his (or her) child realize his potential by achievement of some small goal (like an *A* in second-grade math or a home run for his Little League team) that will seem inconsequential in just a few short weeks or months.

But there is a deeper lesson hidden in this analysis. Spirit is primarily interested in the progress of the spiritual side of your life. Like a parent who may reward a child's accomplishments with candy or a new bicycle as well as love and joy, spirit can and *will* shower you with material blessings as you earnestly strive for spiritual growth. The requirement is roughly the same as the parent–child relationship. No parent will give a child something he knows will detract from the child's growth and development, but he will be quick to give any gift which will obviously be beneficial. So if you can demonstrate to your spirit helpers that money will definitely *aid* your spiritual progress, they will help you attract it in ever-growing waves of prosperity.

A young married man felt he should provide more material and financial blessings for his wife and children. He had started at the bottom in his factory job just three months before, and the economic pressure of four people to support on his modest wage left no margin for error, much less any luxuries. His interest in spiritual progress heightened at about this time, and he reasoned that he could unfold spiritually with much greater effectiveness if his mind weren't so full of the pressures that stem from lack of money. So he began to talk it over with his spirit teachers twice a day. His part of the conversation went something like this: "Beloved teachers, you know I am striving to grow on the spiritual plane, but I need your help. My deep desire to provide a better material life for my family keeps trying to crowd out the spiritual but I realize that both are necessary. Please help me progress in the business world as an aid to my spiritual development. Thank you for your loving help."

Soon he started to get simple ideas of how to do things better on his job. The quality of his work improved as he seemed to apply more creative attention to it, and his sound suggestions to the foreman shortly earned him a substantial raise in pay. He continued to look upon his work as an exercise for spiritual as well as material improvement, and in three short years he progressed all the way to assistant plant superintendent. That is far from the end of his story, but it is enough to illustrate the truth of material progress under the guidance and direction of spirit teachers by a human who is willing to cooperate.

Your path to riches through ever-increasing effectiveness

Seek ye first the kingdom of heaven is the injunction in point. But there is a rule of reason that comes with it. We live in a materially oriented, economic society, so your path to riches must lead through ever-increasing effectiveness in the material world. Improved health is the logical first step. Any day you are not feeling your best, your effectiveness is bound to be lessened. Apply the lessons of our chapter on physical healing and gain evermore radiant health.

Next comes your attitude toward life in general and your work in particular. In all of life, but especially in the business world, there is room for only one emotion. It is that manifestation of positive love that people call *enthusiasm*. Life is an endless series of games by which we strive to attain real spiritual advancement. One of the very important games is the complicated riddle called business. The game attitude gives us the best clue to the most healthy approach toward getting ahead. On the football field it is well known that the enthusiasm generated by desire can make up for a lack of natural ability. Certainly, given two equally matched teams, the one with the greatest *will to win* will put the most points on the scoreboard. We must constantly strive to generate willing enthusiasm for the accomplishment of each assigned task, but it should be tampered by a good gamesman's sense of sportsmanship. Of course, we will gamble and take calculated risks to achieve spectacular gains, but we must abide by the established rules and sound ethical judgment. A spectacular gain that costs us the support of our spirit teachers would be a tragedy! This prompted the Master to remind us, *What profiteth a man to gain the world, but lose his soul?*

Enthusiasm and good sportsmanship will get you maximum mileage from the application of E.S.P. to your work problems. Often there are several possible answers to a business problem, but there is always one *most creative* solution. Since it will benefit the most people, your ability to regularly come up with creative solutions guarantees your continued advancement. Truly creative solutions most often come from your higher self or your spirit teachers. Talk over your business problems alone in your quiet place with your spirit helpers. Explain each problem exactly as you understand it, and ask for creative advice. Then relax and *pay attention!* Sometimes an apparently wild idea will come drifting into your consciousness. Before you dismiss it as ridiculous, talk it out with your spirit helpers; it may have an intensely practical application.

An expediter had a chronic problem getting good quality parts out of several plating shops his company was using. In his quiet place an idea kept pushing its way into his consciousness. At first it seemed to say, "Why don't you set up your own shop?" He knew that his company didn't have nearly enough work to keep a plating shop of its own in operation, and he would have dismissed the idea as worthless, but he paused first to talk it over with his teachers. As he verbalized the question, "How could I sell an idea like this when we obviously don't have the volume for it?" he met with this response: "Why not buy one of your suppliers? You can streamline its operations to do a better job for your company and for its other customers as well." He approached his boss with the idea, and together they went to see the president. A supplier was interested in selling, and our expediter was offered the position of manager of his company's new division. This was only the first of a long series of promotions, each based on one or more creative solutions to chronic problems.

No one can use these ideas for you. But if you pay attention and *apply what you receive,* there is no limit to your progress.

How to set up a current to draw wealth into your life

Seen from the spirit side of life, wealth is as abundant as air or ocean water. Both air and water move in currents, and so does material wealth. You can set up a mental current to draw riches into your life in tidal waves of abundance. The first step is to eliminate those thought patterns which have been blocking the flow of abundance to you. In our last chapter we set out a table of mental poisons and their symptoms. You may have noted references to lack of money as part of the symptoms. Actually, any negative thought pattern will tend to restrict the flow of riches into your experience. Deliberately set out to clear your mental channels of all obstructions to the smooth entry of wealth, now! You should spend at least ten minutes each morning and evening in your quiet place seeking contact with your spirit teachers. During each contact period, ask for guidance and help in ridding yourself of the habit of negative thinking. Then pay attention to the little reminders of the areas where you are falling short, and resolve to improve a little more every day.

A woman of some means had been experiencing an undue amount of financial difficulty. She came to me with the complaint, "I have eliminated all my negative thinking, but my affairs are still in a mess and I seem unable to straighten them out."

As we talked, she explained how she had carefully weeded out her resentment of the people whose efforts had caused her problems, and I agreed she had done this job well. But further discussion clearly revealed a deep-seated fear of financial ruin. Such a strong fear is a very effective prayer for the manifestation of the thing feared, and this was completely negating her positive prayer work. Her efforts to gain new perspective by looking on the whole problem as if it were a checkers game slowly dissolved her mental block and brought about her return to financial peace.

A special area that demands our careful attention is your acceptance of financial responsibility. Some people hate to pay their bills and shirk carrying their share of the financial load in social as well as business situations. This is tantamount to praying for poverty and lack! Learn to *enjoy* paying your bills promptly and fulfilling your obligations graciously. Give thanks to the Infinite Source of all for the abundance you have now, and spend it intelligently. Maintain a neverending vigilance to keep obstructions to the flow of wealth from creeping into your mental environment.

Now that your channels are prepared, let's look to starting the flow of wealth into your personal experience. In the physical world, when you want to get water out of a well, it is necessary to prime the pump. A similar pump-priming is necessary in the mental–spiritual world we seek to master. How do you prime your spiritual pump? Again, we can find our answer by looking at the material world. When you want to get water out of a well, you prime your pump with the same substance, water. So when you want riches, money is the best substance to use in priming your pump. The Christian concept of tithing is an excellent method, but only if it is done with the right attitude. In a very real sense, a farmer tithes when he gives his seed into the loving care of the soil. There is no sense of loss or holding back at planting time because the farmer visualizes the joy of harvest. If you release your tithe to spirit with the same happy expectancy, your harvest will be similarly bountiful.

But some of us may say, "I haven't the resources to tithe, I can barely make ends meet now." That feeling is undoubtedly the cause of your problem, but any attempt to use the law of abundance while harboring such an attitude would be disastrous. If you feel too short to give money, then find a way to give of yourself in loving service. But look forward all the time to the happy day when you can also do your share with plain old-fashioned money.

Spirit has infinite ways of multiplying your goods. Scientific giving is as certain a way to improve your financial lot as modern farming is a way to produce food. As you release each gift in love, you set up an irresistible spiritual current to draw wealth into your experience. It is only necessary to accept without anxiety or greed as the increased flow of riches begins.

A young typist encountered these ideas and decided to give it a try. Instead of the fifty cents she had been dropping into the collection plate on Sundays, she decided she could spare a dollar for openers. Each Sunday for four weeks she made her dollar donation to the church and, sure enough, nothing happened, except that she began to feel better somewhere inside her being. In fact, she felt so good that she decided to increase her weekly donation again, this time to two dollars. As she continued to feel better inside, it reflected in the quality of her work. On the tenth week of her program, an opening developed for a junior executive secretary, and her new radiance and effectiveness led the personnel manager to offer her the position. The thirty-dollar a month raise that came with it made our new secretary so happy that she decided to increase her donation again, this time to three dollars a week. We will summarize the rest of the story, just in case you haven't guessed the outcome. She married the junior executive and taught him the simple secret of her own advancement.

Let spirit express riches in your life

Now you have deliberately set up the current of wealth and it is only necessary to *let* spirit express riches in your life. Build an attitude of gracious acceptance as the happy changes begin to enter your experience. Spirit regularly operates through apparently natural and normal channels. Don't expect the heavens to open up and dump a million gold doubloons on your front porch. Your wealth will seek you through new ideas and opportunities, and it is your responsibility to *pay attention*. It could come from a new train of thought triggered by the chance remark of a friend or even a child.

Act when the spirit impels it! The best idea in the world is no good to anybody until it is put to some practical use. As your idea unfolds, keep asking your teachers what is the best way to implement it. Never brush off an idea because it seems too simple or commonplace. Imagine the value in today's market of a patent on the principle of the safety pin! Or the zipper! There are just as many concepts waiting to be realized today. But your good doesn't have to come in the form of a new product. It could just as easily be a series of individually insignificant ideas about doing your present job better, getting a promotion, or the unfoldment of a completely new career. Know that the tendency of the universal laws is to increase the happiness, health, peace, abundance, and wealth in the lives of all who will cooperate. Use your relaxed awareness to notice and capitalize on your opportunities. Then remember to give thanks, spiritually, mentally, *and financially.*

How to protect yourself from financial harm

In our economically oriented society, it is a truism that any form of harm to you or a member of your family will have some negative effect financially. So it is necessary that we seek protection in its broadest sense. By this time you should be aware of the deeper truth of that wonderful passage: *For He shall give his angels charge over thee, to keep thee in all thy ways. They shall bear thee up in their hands, lest thou dash thy foot against a stone.* (Psalm 91)

You are certain, now, that the *angels* referred to in the psalm are your own spirit teachers. As you earnestly work to cooperate with the great evolutionary plan of the universe, they will provide you with just such protection. You will live the truth of the promise of Psalm 91, *A thousand shall fall at thy side and ten thousand at thy right hand; but it shall not come nigh thee.*

As always, your own efforts provide the small force that is amplified by spirit into an irresistible protective influence which you can place around yourself, your loved ones, and your belongings. In the old occult terminology, you can fashion a "ring-pass-not" which will absolutely prevent the approach of negative occurrences. How do you build your own ring-pass-not?

Our modern world has many examples of effective protection from unwanted conditions and influences. One in particular will help us understand the principle of the ring-pass-not. Many supermarkets, department stores, and other public buildings are air-conditioned; yet their doors stand wide open all day. The cool inner air is protected from invasion by the undesirable outside air by a simple *curtain* of air in motion. This invisible curtain allows normal in-and-out passage to the desirable elements like customers and employees, but it effectively seals out the external heat, smoke, dust, fumes, and smog.

The Heavenly Father provided just such a *curtain* of protection for you. Are you using it? It works quite like the protective air curtain of the supermarket, but it uses currents of thought and living light for its protective shield. *It will work successfully for you,* but only if *you* choose to use it. You must build your own personal consciousness of divine psychic protection.

Start in a quiet moment and visualize a suit of dazzling white light surrounding your body and extending its protective force a foot or more in all directions. Then say to yourself: "The white light of divine protection surrounds me now, sealing out all negative thoughts and experience. Only goodness and purity can penetrate this wonderful light, and I will send nothing but goodness out through it. Thank you, Heavenly Father, for your perfect protection." Now bask in the lovely white light and consciously feel its loving protection. Repeat this simple exercise as often as possible while building your certainty of personal divine protection.

You should renew your protection by using the exercise at least mornings and evenings for the rest of your life. Then any time you feel you are in a tight spot, either physically, mentally, financially, or psychologically, simply call on your teachers and the Heavenly Father to intensify your protective white light. This will not only help you, but will exert a positive influence on all others involved with you. It will take much mental work before your light can give you 100-percent perfect protection, but it will give you some degree of tangible, positive help from the very beginning. Start to practice now! The life you improve is not just your own!

You can extend this protective ring-pass-not to include your home, your automobile, and to some extent the members of your family. The limit to family protection is cooperation in thought from the individuals you wish to protect. Although you can exert some positive influence, every human being is entitled to exercise his own freedom of choice in the matter of accepting such protection.

Let's look at an example of protection of your automobile. Many years ago, after a series of three very minor accidents, I began nurturing the idea of an inch of psychic armor plate around my vehicle. Since that time, I have driven in the extremely heavy Los Angeles area traffic for over twenty years in perfect safety within my inch of *armor plate.* In a couple of emergencies I could swear that another car had been stopped at just that one-inch point, and an accident was averted. There is one exception to the perfect twenty-year record. During one short period of great emotional stress, I decided that this whole spiritual business was a bunch of hogwash, so I dropped my daily renewals of the protective white light. In less than two weeks, I got clobbered in my brand new sports car! I regularly give thanks for this experience. It was the best lesson anyone could ask for. Take it from someone who's been there, this thing really works! And *you* can't afford to be without it.

You can lead a charmed life from now on. The great strength of the whole Judeo–Christian tradition is its generous, loving God who wants only to shower blessings and protection upon His human images. The Master brought us the instruction, *Hitherto have ye asked for nothing: ask, and ye shall receive, that your joy may be full.*

This is one thing that no one can do for you. You must do the asking. Ask the Heavenly Father for the protective white light. Then accept the loving gift, and lead a spiritually charmed life forevermore. Do it now! "The white light of divine protection surrounds me now, sealing out all negative thoughts and experience. Only goodness and purity can penetrate this wonderful light, and I will send nothing but goodness out through it. Thank you, Heavenly Father, for your perfect protection."

How to enjoy your ever-increasing riches

You have paved the way for spirit to manifest ever-growing abundance in your life, so now it is only necessary to learn to enjoy it. This may sound easy, but it is spotted with pitfalls left over from your past attitudes. A man who entered adult life shortly before the great depression of 1929 makes an excellent example of the problem. This man lost his savings when the bank failed, then went for some time without a job when his employer failed. Over the years he learned some of the laws of prosperity, but they were tempered by the vivid memories of the early 1930s. He established a goal of success as $10,000 a year, and attained it reasonably easily; but he could never let himself progress any further. At every meal he kidded about carving very thin slices of meat to be sure there was some left for tomorrow, and his general attitude was one of looking over his shoulder for the coming disaster. By his own standards he was a success, but there was something drastically wrong with his yardstick. He might have progressed so much further into the good life if only he could accept the infinite supply of the Almighty.

As you grow spiritually, it is natural to grow financially also. Don't restrict the wonderful flow of riches by doubting the infinite nature of its source. Accept the flow and use it! Your natural desires are good, and it is good for you and the economy to gratify them. Of course, there is a point of balance between gratification and overindulgence, but your own intelligence will guide you if you pay just a little attention.

Then enjoy paying your bills! Look upon each invoice as a wonderful reminder of God's loving opulence. It is your happy pleasure to keep the flow of riches ever growing and circulating in your life by paying each bill as it becomes due. Mail your checks with a word of thanks to the bountiful Heavenly Father for your many blessings, and watch your goods grow and grow. Let your riches buy you time for things that are uplifting. There can be time for travel and mingling with people of other cultures and religions, for academic or spiritual study, and for those periods of relaxation that precede great spurts of spiritual growth. Relax and enjoy your ever-increasing riches. You will bless many others as well as yourself!

POINTS TO REMEMBER

   I. Money is merely an idea.

  II. Love of money is a good emotion.

 III. Demonstrate to your spiritual teachers that money will aid your spiritual growth.

  IV. Attract your riches through increased personal effectiveness.

   V. Practice creative problem-solving.

  VI. Improve your flow of riches by clearing your mental channels of the old negative blocks.

 VII. Set up a current to attract riches by priming the pump.

VIII. Accept the flow of riches into your life.

  IX. Build your ring-pass-not to protect you from all harm.

   X. Enjoy your ever-increasing riches.

how to
Use E.S.P. to Build
a Dynamic Personality
That Attracts the
Right People

Have you ever noticed how little groups tend to center around certain individuals at a party? You may try to shrug it off, but in your heart you know there is something to it—an intangible something which attracts people in much the same way that moths are attracted to a bright light. You have some of this power now, but you can develop much more. *You can become a center of attention wherever you go!* It is only necessary to learn the simple laws involved.

How to use your psychic centers to extend your personality

The real secret of personal popularity and effectiveness in social and business relationships lies in an ancient saying often blamed on Emerson. It goes something like this: *What you are speaks so loud, I can't hear what you say.* All people are psychic to some extent, although many don't call it that and tend to ignore it. But this is no reason for us to skip over it. Let's restate our proposition for emphasis: *All humans receive psychic impressions from their surroundings,* though this reception is largely unconscious to many people. Many times in your own experience, you have been touched by the obvious sincerity of one new acquaintance or the complete lack of scruples in another. You can be certain now that the feeling was psychically received. Similarly, you are instinctively drawn to some people and quickly form deep and lasting friendships, while it may take months or even years to learn to tolerate others.

Let's examine the psychic reasons for this instinctive behavior as our best approach to gaining control over it. In spite of his reverence for intellect, psychologists insist that modern man is governed by his emotions to a much greater degree than he realizes. We play great games with ourselves trying to believe that our major decisions are based on sound intellectual judgment, but we rush into getting married or purchasing homes, cars, or minks without so much as a shred of reason to support our actions. This is not necessarily bad, it is simply a fact worthy of careful contemplation. How long has it been since you got good and mad at somebody? Now that you have had time to cool off, you can see the tremendous power of emotion to cloud or completely obscure intellectual reasoning. Now what is that power? Does it have other effects on us?

This brings us right back to the psychic centers. Your own psychic centers are active twenty-four hours of every day. They constantly send and receive the vibratory energy which is the power of emotion. Your aura is a field of the blended energies from each of your centers, and it is regularly changed by your changing thought and emotional patterns. It is also affected by similar patterns in people with whom you come in close contact. Physical proximity to another person naturally brings your auras closer together, and your emotional reactions to each other are the result of the harmonic blending of these vibrations in the case of pleasant relationships or dissonance when the relationships are negative. Certainly you have at least one friend whose very presence is a comfort to you. You may have thought it silly to feel that way, but there is a sound basis in fact for it. Some auras react upon each other to produce emotional and psychological peace of much greater quality than either person seems able to attain alone. It falls in with that interesting promise of the Master: *Where two or three are gath-*

ered together in my name, there will I be also. Don't hesitate to enjoy such relationships without reservation; it will advance the spiritual progress of all concerned.

What of the few persons whose presence seems to make you tense and uncomfortable? Some auras don't naturally blend with each other without the conscious effort of at least one of the parties. It is reasonable to avoid contact with people whose presence makes you uncomfortable. But you should look forward to the day when you learn to adjust your own aura to compensate for the difference in vibration. Still it may require substantial effort to adjust your aura enough to remain comfortable in the presence of one who is intensely self-centered and materially grasping. This may help us to understand why we seldom receive physical visits from our own spirit teachers. They certainly want to give us all the encouragement and help we need, but to bring their highly refined auras too close to our relatively coarse ones must make them just as uncomfortable as some lesser-developed humans make us. Give extra thanks next time you are aware of a spirit teacher's presence, and strive to purify your thoughts and aura as much as possible to help make your friend's stay more pleasant. The same basic techniques used to adjust your aura apply to making a visiting spirit or a visiting earthly person comfortable. It is the secret of making other people like you.

How to make other people like you

Regardless of your opinion of them or their station in life, it is to your advantage to be liked by as many people as possible. Others' feelings about you do have an effect on your aura. The positive feelings are helpful, of course, but any negative vibrations must be continually cleansed out of your being if you are to remain at maximum effectiveness. The less negativity that impinges upon you, the less energy that must be wasted in purifying your aura, and the more you will have left for constructive accomplishments.

The universe tends to return your basic projections as the pattern of your own daily experience, so let's start by examining the sort of vibrations you project into your surroundings. It should be obvious that the more positive the emanations from your aura, the more pleasant will be the response from your environment. The sincere, confident approach to life is the most effective way to tune your psychic centers for this purpose. You may hide your true feelings from the conscious minds of others, but you can't keep from projecting them into the great psychic stream from which everyone receives impressions. *There is no escaping it!* If you expect people to be comfortable around you, you must project sincere goodwill at all times. There are no shortcuts, no gimmicks, and no pills that will do it for you. But a habit of genuine goodwill toward all your fellow beings will bring you many side blessings while truly making everyone like you.

Projecting genuine goodwill is the first half of the battle, and it will give excellent results just by itself. But let's also consider a more positive use of your E.S.P. in this area. If you could tune in to the other's moods by sensing the projections of his psychic centers, wouldn't you know just what to say and do to achieve the maximum positive response? You already have a tool to do just that! Use your rapidly developing clairsentience to tune in on the other's psychic wavelength. Everyone has some experience in sensing another's moods, but you will increase in accuracy and sensitivity as you apply your conscious attention to this very practical psychic application.

As you sense your friend's mood, a combination of intuition and good judgment will lead you to adjust your own projections to blend and harmonize. You will make a substantial contribution to the goodwill of the world by spreading peace, happiness, encouragement, and joy by entering into the spirit of applied psychic goodwill. Give of yourself to promote the good of those around you. Provide the light touch that gently kids a comrade out of a bad mood or helps him adjust to a personal disappointment.

Build the habit of psychically seeking the best method to bring out the good in your associates. There is no better way to add to your own good than by seeking good for others. Pay attention to your clairsentient impulses and act on them for the upliftment of everyone you contact. Often you will find that helping someone else involves selling an idea.

How to sell an idea

The first principle of selling an idea is communication. Most often an idea has to be sold because your friend has a psychic or emotional block to clear thinking in his problem area. The direct approach is seldom effective, as typified by the old adage, "A woman convinced against her will is a woman unconvinced." And that is equally true of men. If you would effectively reach your friend, it must be from a position of psychic rapport. Similarly in the commercial world, a salesman will attempt the psychologically symbolic act of sitting on the same side of the desk as his prospect in order to create the impression that both of them are on the same team, rather than being adversaries. You will rarely sell anything as an adversary, but the job is easy from a position of psychic rapport. Take the time to build it with friendly topical conversation. Then begin a friendly game of verbal fencing while your conversation skirts the fringes of your main point.

A computer salesman's approach to one particular office manager is a good illustration of the technique. During most of the period in question, the office had no machines of the salesman's make, but operated about thirty competitive machines standardized as to model and style. The salesman's first visit was strictly a get-acquainted contact where he probed for future conversational material. Then on each subsequent visit he opened with friendly questions about the office manager's family and the progress of his son in the Little League. On his second visit he inquired about maintenance problems and downtime on the existing computers. On his third visit he sold the company some peripheral software which proved to be slightly better than what was in regular use. It was almost five months before he got around to leaving a demonstrator of his latest model, and all this time he kept the personal relationship uppermost in the conversation. Eventually he replaced every competitive computer with his own by clearly demonstrating the savings in repair cost and lost time to be gained from his product. The toughest part of his job was in overcoming the office manager's emotional resistance to change and to admitting that he might have made a mistake in standardizing with the other line in the first place. This could only be accomplished by indirectly approaching the subject, so the office manager never had to admit even a hint of an error.

Note the details of the technique. Send your message psychically while your conversation skirts the main issue. Carefully avoid statements or implications that your prospect is completely wrong about anything. Instead, lead him slowly to see that there is a potential benefit to him by opening his mind to a new idea. When he is finally interested in exploring the new idea, ask a leading question like: "Why don't you try it?" Or in the case of our computer salesman: "How about my bringing a demonstrator for you to play around with for a couple of weeks?"

You are a master of the art when you can get your prospect to verbalize the idea as an outgrowth of your carefully directed discussion. Then praise him as if the idea were really his own. You don't have to take credit for a good idea as long as it is actually hatched. People like to believe they are doing their own thinking whether it is true or not. Let them, as long as it helps. But remember that this technique should be used only if you are genuinely interested in the other's welfare. Otherwise, your lack of sincerity will reach your friend's psychic centers and eventually give you away. Always be sincere and work to help your associates tactfully but effectively.

How to attract the right people and opportunities

Your sincere desire to be a positive influence in the lives of all who come into your sphere of activity is the secret of attracting the right people and opportunities. As you seek to bring light and happiness to others, your spirit band will seek the same for you. They are particularly interested in your happiness as an aid to your further spiritual evolution.

Thus you can see that when you are experiencing great happiness, the best way to insure its continuation is to give thanks and pray for continued spiritual growth. The bumps and hard places in life jog us back onto the spiritual pathway by reminding us of the extremely precarious nature of our physical existence. When we stray from the path of growth, life will keep bumping us harder and harder; and only as we seek spirit do we begin to find respite.

But you have a personal contact with His *angels* now. Go into your quiet place and talk over your needs with these spirit helpers. They are real friends, and you can kid with them just like any other people. If anything, their sense of humor is better developed than ours, and a good joke often works to improve your contact. I have felt closer to a particular teacher for a long time because of the running bit of banter we carried on for the two years it took to complete our first book. Relax and enjoy good fellowship with your spirit friends, and ask them for help. Then observe the little indications of its forthcoming. Since our channels of communication are not yet as effective as those between occupants of physical bodies, you won't necessarily understand exactly how spirit intends to help you. But if you remain alert, expecting help and guidance, it will always be there at the right time.

A widow sat down to talk over her problems with her spirit teachers. She expressed her feelings like this: "Look here, friends, the children have grown up and left the nest, and things are pretty lonely for me. There must be a good man who needs warmth and companionship as much as I do. Please help us find each other." She lost count of the number of weeks she daily repeated her request for help, but she never lost hope. Then one Sunday in church her meditation was interrupted by what felt like a sharp electric shock. She looked in the direction of the energy *source* and found herself staring into the eyes of a man in the row in front of her and two seats to the left. She smiled and returned to her meditation. Instantly she received an impression that she should arrive early for the next few services and be sure to get the same seat. She carefully made it to her seat next Sunday, and again felt an electric shock just as the same man found the seat next to her. Again she smiled, and they exchanged a few pleasantries before the service. By the fourth Sunday he asked her to join him for coffee before going home. It wasn't what we would call a whirlwind courtship, but it did develop into a warm and happy marriage that has added much pleasantness to the later years of both these wonderful people.

Notice that, as always, the spirit forces guide and help, but you must follow up with your own best efforts to manifest the desired results. One young man had been out of work for three weeks before he realized he could ask for spirit help. Finally he went to his quiet place and talked to his teachers: "Somewhere there must be a job that needs me as much as I need it. Please, my teachers, help us find each other." As he started on his daily round of job seeking, he just missed the bus, so he decided to walk along to the next stop to help pass the time. Along the way a local newspaper that he seldom read caught his eye and he was impelled to pick it up. He was still looking at the new batch of help wanted ads as he boarded the bus. He noticed a particular ad just as his bus reached the corner mentioned in the paper. He hopped off, rushed into the building, and was hired, almost before he realized what was happening.

Your spirit friends are always ready to help you. And you understand the truth that you help each other by cooperating in positive undertakings. Nothing is too big or small to deserve help from spirit, but only if you are doing your best to help yourself. Give it a try!

How to cope with difficult personalities

Now you are doing beautifully, attracting new and interesting people and opportunities into your experience. But every once in awhile you seem to attract someone who proves very difficult to get along with. How do you handle yourself?

First, adjust your attitude toward the situation. Be thankful for this wonderful new opportunity to demonstrate your mastery over problems which have previously plagued you. Next, understand that the reason you rub each other the wrong way is an inharmonious blending of your auras. Obviously you can't expect to change your adversary's aura, but you have now learned to adjust your own. The secret is in your preparations *before* you deliberately enter the proximity of such a person. When you know a meeting is imminent, arrange to be alone for a minute, if only in the bathroom. Consciously call on your spirit teachers for help in controlling your reactions and adjusting your psychic centers to produce the changes in your aura that will help blend with the other's and protect you from any negative influence. Then mentally will your psychic centers to adjust under your teachers' direction. Now set your own attitude. Remember that no matter how offensive a person may seem to you, he is an expression of the same God and the same life that you are. Mentally salute the God-self in the other, put on your warmest smile, and walk out to your meeting.

If you are caught off guard by a chance meeting, mentally go through the whole process while you are exchanging greetings. Use your smile liberally, and constantly keep in mind the simple fact that it takes two people to disagree or argue. Here is a perfect opportunity to practice selling your ideas. You will never be sure of your effectiveness in this area until you can consistently sell your sound ideas to the acquaintances you consider the most difficult. You can enjoy a happy relationship with anyone you meet if you will take the trouble to make it that way.

A company had contracts with several unions but seemed to be having particular difficulty with a small local which covered only a dozen of its employees. There was a running battle for almost two years which consumed enormous amounts of time for both sides. Every meeting seemed to break up with threats and bitterness, and strike preparations were under way almost constantly. When a new beef developed over the company's refusal to take a man sent over by the union hiring hall, the young vice president decided to attend this meeting along with his usual set of negotiators. Just before leaving the office, he sat for a few minutes in the restroom making his mental preparations. He asked his spirit teachers for help, and resolved to see only the God-self in the business agents throughout the meeting. His friendly smile and warm handshake started things off on the right foot, and he seemed inspired to say exactly the right thing at every tense moment in the discussions. At the end of a two-hour meeting, the union representatives were convinced that the company had acted in good faith, and a friendly ending to a meeting took place for the first time. This marked the beginning of a long period of relations between the two sides, all because somebody took the trouble to be spiritually prepared for a difficult meeting.

You can win understanding and sympathetic consideration from *anybody* if you will conscientiously use what you know. Never hesitate to call on your spirit friends for help. Helping you helps them also! Let spirit participate in making your daily round of experiences more pleasant for you and everyone you contact. It's fun and profitable, too!

The give and take of real friendship

Now that we can get over the rough spots, let's take a look at what we should expect from a real friendship. When auras naturally blend and produce the happy sensation of effortless comfort to another's presence, you have discovered the basis for a deep and lasting friendship. True friendship is characterized by the absence of dependence or need. It is a special relationship for the simple sharing of experiences which enrich both lives in the process. It is the same with earthly or spirit friendships; the sharing of experiences and mutual striving for growth and the good of mankind help all parties.

Either an earthly or a spirit friendship can of itself be an expression of the mystic experience. When auras blend in the deeper relationships, the light of each is strengthened, and a new plateau of spiritual consciousness may be attained. Sitting in near darkness with your friend, you may actually light up the room, or produce such a spiritual vibration that one of the higher spirits can bring a special manifestation. Your totally unselfish admiration for each other may lead to a momentary flash of consciousness where you literally think and feel, not as yourself, but *as your friend.* Welcome any such sensation, because the surest way to the experience of complete oneness with God is directly through the ability to think and feel as someone else. The ability can then be expanded so you think and feel as the whole planet, and finally the universe; and thus you find the ultimate in spiritual companionship with the God-presence itself. We will discuss the mystic experience in detail in Chapter 9, but let's close this section with one quick brush at how to find a true friend.

The secret of finding true friendship lies in your answer to the question: What do you expect to get out of a friendship? If you are looking for material gain, prestige, or the like, you must realize you aren't seeking true friendship at all. But if you can say you want just the happy sharing of warmth and unselfish affection for the sheer joy of the experience, you undoubtedly have many friends already. So you'd like to have more? O.K. If you don't hide in a box under the stairs all day, you must regularly find yourself around people. They are your new friends. Treat them that way! Greet everyone you encounter with a warm smile and a friendly hello.

For those who say, "I don't dare smile at strangers because it will probably be misinterpreted," there is an obvious answer. *Nobody will misinterpret your smile unless you want him to!* We all respond pleasantly to someone else's warmth, but we are still ready to give it *all the respect it requires.* The way to find a friend is to give friendship. All strangers are made of the same God-essence you are, so they must be friends already. It's just that you haven't found out yet. Treat everybody that way and you will never be lonely. You will never want for true friendship either.

POINTS TO REMEMBER

    I. You can become a center of attention wherever you go.

    II. You constantly send and receive psychic impressions through your aura and psychic centers.

    III. Psychological comfort or discomfort in another's presence depends on the degree of blending of your auras.

    IV. Project genuine goodwill to everyone you meet.

    V. Let your clairsentience guide you in sensing others' moods and blending harmoniously with them.

    VI. Ask for spirit help in attracting the people and opportunities you need.

    VII. You can learn to adjust your aura to blend with difficult people.

    VIII. To find a friend, give friendship.

how to
Find the Strength
to Face Any Crisis

Our workday world gets much pleasure and respite by poking good-natured fun at itself. One of my favorite expressions of office humor is the little sign that says: "If you can remain calm while all around you people are screaming and tearing their hair, you just don't understand the situation!"

There may be much truth to that little slogan, but there is another kind of calm which results from knowing *more* than those who panic. This *more* gives us all the strength we need to face any crisis. Let's start building our strength with a look at the sources of stress and the havoc they often cause.

Why some people crack under stress

Whether you like it or not, God is the substance and very life of your being. Some people refuse to accept this simple fact, and so build up an illusion of separation from God. They think of their being as bearing the same sort of relationship to God that a fountain pen bears to the engineer who designed it. Thus they feel isolated and on their own, and they have nothing to fall back on when the going gets rough. They expect about as much help from God as if they were a fountain pen praying to its designer for help after being stepped on. So that's what they get.

Our study of the psychic energy centers shows that we are much more intimately connected to the universe and our fellow creatures than any materially oriented individual could realize. We understand that the rest of the world tends to treat us exactly as we expect it to in the depths of our own being. Thus we recognize that we attract all our own bad breaks as well as the good ones that so regularly come to us. We easily understand that guilt and fear are deadly negative prayers which summon bad breaks with irresistible power. So we strive daily to rid our mental and emotional lives of all negativity. And we are making real progress! But nobody is immune to the sin of backsliding. We get all wrapped up in the apparent importance of our own little sphere of activity, and literally forget to keep our perspective. So we lapse back into some of the old negative patterns, and cry out in anguish when we begin to reap the disastrous results.

If you have allowed the illusion of separateness from God to creep back into your being, you are in a very miserable state. When things look hopeless and the world seems to be closing in on you, where will you turn? Some people reach the breaking point and crack under the stress. Our mental hospitals and psychiatrists' couches are full of them. But there is no need to let this happen to you. Turn back to God as the only real source of personal strength, and you will make it safely through the most difficult situations.

How to find your source of personal strength

Down through the ages, people have found their greatest strength in the same place. It comes from an unshakable faith in God, such as that which prompted the psalmist of old to exclaim: *I will lift up mine eyes unto the hills from whence cometh my help. My help cometh from the Lord, which made heaven and earth. He will not suffer thy foot to be moved: he that keepeth thee will not slumber.* (Psalm 121:1-3)

Even before you embarked upon this earthly life, He gave His angels charge over you. In the work of our second chapter you met your own guardian angels. We most often call them our spirit teachers, but regardless of the label, they are an ever-present source of tangible help in any emergency. They have helped you many times in the past, whether you are aware of it or not, and the variety of their methods is infinite. A devoted student of this work told me the following story in complete sincerity:

> Last year while I was still driving cross-country trucks, I had an excellent demonstration of spirit protection. Late at night I got very sleepy, so I pulled my rig off the road to take a short nap. It happened that I stopped at the top of a long grade, and I must not have set the brake properly. I woke up with a start to see that my truck was careening down the hill at terrific speed. But my fear quickly vanished as I noticed the shadowy form of a powerful Indian handling the steering with a skill that was obviously out of this world. He kept the truck on the road around a couple of wild curves and finally brought it to a stop in a safe place on the shoulder. I had seen Tomahawk in my meditations before, but this was my first obvious demonstration of his physical protection. I am sure I owe him my life from that instance, and I feel his presence now every time I get at the wheel of a motor vehicle. He is a constant source of physical protection.

This is not such an unusual story. Normal people are helped by the spirit world in countless ways every day. A middle-aged woman was walking home from an evening church meeting. As she passed a tall hedge, she found herself looking right into the muzzle of a revolver. The voice said, "Let's have that purse," but it was interrupted by a flash of blue light, like a tiny lightning bolt, which knocked the gun to the pavement. The bandit fled in terror, and the woman hurried home to give thanks to her spirit helpers in the safety of her own sanctum.

A young boy was swimming alone in a secluded bay. As often seems the case for young boys, he overestimated his prowess and soon found himself over his head and sinking from panic and exhaustion. Suddenly a hand grabbed his trunks and lifted him just out of the water. He was transported in this fashion back to where the water came up only to his waist and deposited back on his feet by the invisible hand.

These are not *pipe dreams,* they are natural examples of the help you can expect when you are working in tune with your spirit teachers. You earn special protection by spiritual striving, and by consciously working with your spirit band. You are privileged to stop at any time and return to the capricious rule of the law of averages, but very few who have tasted this protection do. If you haven't yet started to seek contact with your teachers, *now* is the best time!

How to understand your stresses

Most of us would agree that life on this Earth is very much like a chess game. Your various activities correspond to your chess pieces, and you move them about trying to gain an advantage. But the rest of the world seemingly acts as your opponent and tries to counter your moves. All the stresses in life result from frustration and disappointment arising out of our own poor moves or the excellent moves of our opponent. This is the simple reality of life until you *decide to change your relationship to it*.

There are two ways to work from this analogy to alleviate our stresses. We called it a chess *game*. Now if you can really understand life that way, you will realize that it isn't a tremendous tragedy to lose a game once in awhile. This can be a mighty help in regaining your perspective, no matter how bad a pickle you manage to get yourself into. But most of us also like to win our share, so let's get back to the board and play. We started out by looking at the whole world as the opponent, but an old saying is in point here. It goes: "If you can't beat 'em, join 'em." The world will remain your opponent *until you choose to join it*. What are you trying to accomplish anyway?

Instead of trying to scratch a living out of a hostile world, a small change of perspective can do wonders for your peace of mind. Why not adopt a basic purpose to work for the good of mankind? Of course, you still have to work! Man needs the honest sense of accomplishment that comes from a day's job well done. But what of your attitude? A man who has scratched hard for a living comes home weary and discouraged at the end of his day. But another man who worked on the same job all day for the benefit of his fellow men, comes home with a smile on his face, a song in his heart, and the same wage in his pocket. The *reason* you do a job, and your *attitude* toward it, have a lot more to do with the fatigue factor than the actual amount of physical energy you expend. Check your feelings on the way to work each morning. Be sure you have the right attitude and perspective!

Often we think we need help when we really need only to correct our approach to the problem. Then we get disgusted with our God and our spirit teachers because we are not rescued by some spectacular supernormal intervention. It is important that you learn to recognize the times when you actually need help. In times of genuine need you can take comfort in the unbreakable promise of the Lord: *Before they call, I will answer; and while they are yet speaking, I will hear.* (Isaiah 65:24)

You will never be forsaken by His angels! They may let you stay in the uncomfortable situation you have built for yourself just long enough to be sure you learn your lesson, but they will never let you come to lasting harm. When the world seems to be closing in on you, go to your quiet place and call on your spirit teachers for help. Then sit in the silence until you get the response. But don't be surprised if the answer is, "You are perfectly capable of working this out for yourself." A significant part of your mission on Earth is to learn your own mastery over physical and material conditions. Tangible help when you don't need it would be weakening, so this you will not receive. But when the chips are down, and your best is not good enough, you are in the same position as Jesus when He said: *Thinkest thou that I cannot now pray to my Father, and he shall presently give me more than twelve legions of angels?* (Matt. 26:53) Let that be your faith also.

A teenage girl was exploring a small cave alone. She tripped on a timber and caused a collapse of part of the roof, apparently trapping herself inside. In the utter darkness she knelt to pray. Soon tender hands lifted her to her feet and guided her faltering steps around two small bends to a brush-covered hole just big enough to climb out. If you have *faith,* the Father will send *more* than twelve legions of angels when you need them.

How to ask for help for others

The further you progress in this work, the less apt you are to need help for yourself, and the more you will want to seek help for others. This sharing of our spiritual blessings is an essential requisite to further growth. As always, sincerity and faith are the two greatest keys. Let's look at the methods of the Master.

Jesus often brought healing help by the laying on of hands or some other form of definite physical contact. Follow His example and practice the healing work you started in Chapter 3. But the true catalyst in all His ministry was the Master's great faith, which is perhaps most clearly demonstrated before the tomb of Lazarus:

Then they took away the stone from the place where the dead was laid. And Jesus lifted up his eyes, and said, Father, I thank thee that thou hast heard me. And I knew that thou hearest me always: but because of the people which stand by I said it, that they may believe that thou hast sent me. And when he thus had spoken, he cried with a loud voice, Lazarus, come forth. And he that was dead came forth. . . . (John 11:38-44)

In more modern times, the great Hindu leader, Mahatma Gandhi, used a somewhat different approach to helping others. He entered the silence to pray for help, then demonstrated his faith by announcing a personal fast until his prayer was answered. His spiritual leadership was the inspiration behind the birth of the great nation India. You will gain much by entering your quiet place to ask your teachers for help in understanding the deep faith of such a spiritual man. Then strive to build an equal faith in *you*.

The simple trust in the power of God demonstrated by a grandmother brought many blessings to the people around her. She talked to God in her room, in the garden, and even on the streetcar, regularly asking help for her neighbors. All the neighborhood animals were her friends, including two little mice who occupied a hole in the wall of her room. She fed them and prayed for their welfare also. Her faithful prayers healed a dying rosebush, and produced the most beautiful camellias in the city. She was so close to God that her very presence had a healing effect on anyone in need. When she passed on, she was missed by people and animals alike. Do whatever is necessary to satisfy your intellect and build a faith like that—it is worth more than all the material possessions you might accumulate!

How do *you* ask for help for others? Go into your quiet place and greet your spirit teachers. Talk over your friend's needs as you would with someone on Earth, and ask for spirit help. Then *according to your faith* it is done! *Believe* that God is helping your friend through the agency of the spirit world and *it is so*. Then give thanks. Know that spirit is working to bring the highest good into the lives of all concerned. With this technique you can obviously do no harm, and the potential good is beyond the limits of human imagination. Never refuse to ask for help for anyone in need. The asking will truly benefit you both.

The secret of getting help for yourself

It's relatively easy to ask for help for someone else, because the question of whether you deserve it doesn't get in the way. But the first thought that hits most of us when we feel we need personal assistance is, "Am I worthy of it?" It seems that we can remember our every shortcoming just when we need help the most.

Modern psychologists call this *guilt*, and it is the most destructive commodity in the universe. The first thing a mentally healthy person learns is not to carry a grudge against any fellow person, but we somehow forget to apply that to ourselves. There is a beautiful passage in the Lord's Prayer which bears directly on this: *And forgive us our trespasses, as we forgive those who trespass against us.* You are entitled to forgiveness from the universe in the same measure that you forgive others for real or fancied wrongs against you. Meditate upon this carefully. Then proceed to honestly and fervently forgive anyone and everyone who may have wronged you. Now claim your own forgiveness! Remember, the Master came to show the way, not to chastise or condemn. Even on the cross He said, *Father, forgive them. . . .* Go before your spirit teachers in your quiet place and claim your forgiveness for everything that seems to stand in the way of your worthiness.

Once you have dissolved the blocks of guilt, the only limit to progress is your own faith. A living faith must be built on a sound base of understanding, and it should be renewed by twice daily contacts with your spirit teachers. Each time you sit in your quiet place and receive a positive response to your call, the reality of the spirit side of life becomes more to you. Strengthen and renew your ties with your spirit teachers throughout the good periods of life, so you can count on their help when you really need it.

How do you go about asking for help? How can you be sure you are heard? Any time or place you are accustomed to talking to your teachers, you can be sure they are there, and *they will hear you!* Tell them your problems and the extent of your efforts to solve them. Demonstrate that you are doing everything within your power to achieve the solution with your own efforts. Then ask for that little extra push from spirit which is certain to tip the scales in your favor. Feel your teachers' response, and *believe* they are helping you. Then, according to your faith, you will receive whatever you need the most. Let's look at a detailed approach to some typical situations.

How to get a new job

At some time or other, each of us has the feeling that the secret of all our future personal happiness lies in landing a new job. This is a time of special crisis, and we should begin with a careful assessment of the factors which have put us in this uncomfortable situation. Whether you are out of work or just plain miserable at your present job, there is a deep lesson to be learned *before* you blindly strike out on a job hunt. All of life's bumps come to teach us some special lessons and we will be stuck with our problem until we wake up enough to digest its inner meaning.

The place to start is in your quiet place, meditating on the lesson to be drawn from your difficulty. The question to ask is: "What are the qualities or attitudes in me that have brought me to this uncomfortable situation?" or "How did I go about attracting this?" When I am in difficulty, I have to find the key and *change something within me* in order to accomplish the cure. Ask the question of your higher self and your teachers, then *pay attention* to the answer. This is no time to rationalize and make up all sorts of excellent excuses. The only way you can claim the power to extricate yourself is to admit it was your misuse of your power that got you into this fix in the first place.

A man was on the verge of quitting his vice presidency of a small but rapidly growing corporation. For several months it had seemed that his efforts were not appreciated and somehow it was all for naught anyway. Before taking any action, he retired to his quiet place and asked the key question: "What is there in me that makes my job seem such a waste of energy?" In the peace of his silence the following train of thought unfolded: "Because of your intense interest in spiritual things, you will never achieve the depths of satisfaction from your job that most executives do; *but you do have an obligation* to your family, and it will be to your spiritual advantage to continue ful-filling it. Your satisfaction is to be attained from helping other people and your executive position gives you the wherewithal and opportunity to bring inspiration and tangible help to many. You need a change of attitude, not a change of job! If you switch jobs in your present frame of mind, the next one may turn out to be even more miserable."

He took his lesson to heart, buckled down on the job, and eventually amassed a fortune sufficient to retire to a happy life of philanthropy.

Another man who was out of work got quite a different answer. The voice within him said, "Your cynical attitude toward your employer and your immediate supervisor lowered the quality of your work so much you had to be fired. It's time for you to adopt a completely positive approach, clean yourself up mentally and psychologically, get off your fanny, and go looking for your new job, *now!*"

Only when you understand the lesson of your situation are you ready for spirit help in correcting the physical and material aspect of it. When you feel you understand, send your call for help loud and clear. Say, "Beloved teachers, I'm doing my best to assimilate my lesson and change for the better. Now please help me find just the right spot to unfold more of my talents in loving service to mankind."

Then keep the faith! Do everything you know how to help yourself, and you can be certain that spirit will come through with all the extra help you need, now and forevermore!

How to find your perfect mate

Marriage is one of the least understood of our major institu-tions. Regardless of our age, education, or emotional maturity, we tend to rush into it blindly, then spend years suffering or trying to patch it up. Our psychologists and marriage coun-selors preach constantly that the key to a successful union is *compromise,* but there is a higher truth that is worthy of careful examination. Compromise will certainly make a bad situation more comfortable, but a marriage with little compromise is infinitely more desirable. Your ideal mate is so completely in tune with you spiritually, mentally, and psychologically that compromise is rarely necessary.

The idea of compromise assumes initial disagreement and infers some pushing and pulling at each other. If you are already married in a less than ideal relationship, I certainly don't advise a bunch of hasty actions. Each individual situation carries its own set of special obligations, and differences should be resolved along carefully directed spiritual lines. But if you are single, and looking forward to marriage sometime in the future, *take heed*.

There is a great deal of truth to the old idea that marriages are made in heaven. The good ones really are! But many times the most completely unlikely people find some attraction for each other and confuse it with love. They get a silly idea that the simple act of a marriage ceremony will somehow dissolve all their differences and they will "live happily ever after." This is one of the areas where we need the most help from our spirit teachers. If you already have your eye on a potential partner, bear with us for just a little way while we discuss that important preliminary.

Your own quiet place is the best base of operations for the seeking of a soul mate. Call on your teachers and talk it over with them. Tell them of your desire for true spiritual love and marriage, and tell them what you expect to bring to your mate. Listen to the little impressions that warn you of too much selfishness in your dreams of the ideal marriage, and work to polish and beautify your concept. Then ask for guidance and help in locating your ideal mate. Know that somewhere there is another person whose being will blend perfectly with yours in the creation of an ideal marriage, and that this person is seeking you even as you are seeking him.

Then go to places where people of like nature to your own are likely to be attracted. If you are religiously inclined, the church of your choice is an excellent place to meet new friends. Or try a course in night school, the neighborhood little theater, civic activities, or charitable work. Wear your friendly smile and be easy to meet. Any new friend may be the instrument of your introduction to your soul mate. Sooner than you dare expect, you will meet someone you think (or hope) is the wonderful mate you are seeking. As the acquaintance begins to warm into friendship or infatuation, you are nearing the crisis point where spirit help is most important.

With your teachers' help, you must decide if this is your soul mate, or if you should just keep right on looking. Understand that *unless you are a saint,* it would be a grave mistake to contemplate marrying one. The real question is, do your faults and weaknesses blend along with your strengths? Do you want to change the other person? Or does he want to change you? If you are interested in the other for anything except exactly what he (or she) is right now, forget it! Go into your quiet place and ask your teachers if you are glossing over anything in the other's character or personality that will be unbearable in the long run. Are you relaxed and comfortable at just being yourself in your potential mate's company? Does he pay attention to you when you are out with other people? And vice-versa? Could you just sit back to back for an hour without talking and feel uplifted by the warm glow of the blending of your auras?

Listen to your higher self and your spirit teachers; they are not blinded by the strange workings of body chemistry we so often mistake for love. A natural blending of spirit and aura, completely without the necessity for compromise, is the ideal state. And *it is attainable on our earth.* You settle for less at the risk of years of tugging and compromise. Marriage is a classic example of the value of *quality* as opposed to quantity.

I don't necessarily subscribe to the theory that there is only one soul mate for each of us, but I'm certain that for every one individual who would make you a good soul mate, there are at least a million who would make you a lousy marriage partner. Without spirit guidance, *you are not equipped to make a wise decision* in the heat of a courtship. Go into your quiet place and commune with your spirit teachers as often and as long as necessary to be sure you are not heading into a disaster. *Spirit guidance is real and it will never fail you!* This may be the time it is hardest to do so, but it is to your best advantage to pay attention to the voices of those whose vision is clear.

How to get instant help in an emergency

There was a terrible screeching of brakes, and two automobiles that had apparently been bound to wind up as a tangled mass of metal stopped fractions of an inch apart. So instead of becoming a stretcher case, the young salesman met a corporation president who offered him an excellent chance as his new sales manager. Not disaster, but new opportunity! This man seemed to lead a charmed life, and so can you.

All life as we know it on Earth is maintained by an extremely delicate balance of seemingly hostile forces. Without the insulating effect of the atmosphere, we would burn to death in the sun during the day, then freeze in the darkness at 200 degrees or more below zero. Every day we read of individual lives snuffed out by literally thousands of different methods, yet many of them were in the very prime of their usefulness to society. If the world's great poets, doctors, authors, and scientists don't naturally receive special protection from the spirit agencies, why should we expect that *you* can?

The answer is contained in the question itself. Because you dare to *expect it,* spirit help is available to you. Of course, there is the inevitable price. We never get something for nothing, even from spirit. The price for complete spirit protection is your sincere and steady effort to work with the spirit world in uncovering your "mission" in life and unfolding your greatest potential for good to the whole of mankind. Don't wait until it's too late to put on the brakes! Start earning your spirit protection now. In a very real sense we each have a spiritual bank account, much like a checking account in a commercial bank anywhere in the United States. The primary rule for using such an account is *you can't take out more than you put in.*

If you haven't already, *now* is just the right time to start making twice daily deposits to your spiritual account in the peaceful atmosphere of your own quiet place. In a broader sense, the spiritual communion in your quiet place will begin to color your whole life with a richer understanding of people, and you will be impelled to shine your light to help them over the dark spots. As you devote more attention to the world of spirit, you will notice more and more evidence of tangible spirit help in your routine affairs. Give thanks for it and resolve to earn more of the same. We will begin the search for your mission in the next chapter.

POINTS TO REMEMBER

   I. The illusion of separateness from God robs people of the emotional strength to handle stress.

  II. Faith in God is the source of all personal strength.

 III. Stress is caused by our wrong attitudes toward the world.

 IV. Spirit protection is tangible and sometimes dramatic in its handling of emergencies.

  V. Spirit will never forsake you.

 VI. You are richly blessed by sharing your spirit help with others.

VII. Your honest striving and faith in your spirit teachers guarantee all the help you need.

VIII. Work with your spirit teachers and build a charmed life.

how
E.S.P. Can Reveal
Your True Reason
for Living

Step outside on any clear night and look up at the myriad of stars shining in the great nothingness we call the sky. Science tells us that each star you see is really another sun, probably much bigger than ours and quite possibly surrounded by orbiting planets like this one. The magnitude of the universe remains beyond the ability of our intellect to encompass, yet in all its vastness, it seems to be made of the infinite repetition of a few simple patterns. No matter how complex the organism or galaxy, it is made up of nature's basic building blocks, all assembled according to logical patterns.

From the submicroscopic world of atoms and molecules to the marvelous Milky Way, man looks at nature's patterns and ponders his own meaning.

The age-old question, "Why am I here?"

One of the major characteristics which distinguishes man from the lower animals is his ability to objectively contemplate his own nature and seek a meaning and purpose for his existence. Man has asked this burning question since he first began to think, "Why am I here?" Brilliant philosophers have devised a fantastic multiplicity of answers based on sound logic and monumental soarings of reason. No matter what your inclination, you can find someone's philosophical system that will help you for a time. But philosophy somehow seems to get bound up in an intricate series of mental gymnastics until the poor struggling student gets ready to accept the old jibe that goes something like, "An expert is a person who knows more and more about less and less, until finally he knows everything about nothing, and becomes a philosopher." Things aren't really that bad, but it is certainly true that no purely mental system can lead you to the *personal experience* of meaning in your own life.

Jesus had a stimulating answer to our basic "why." He said, *I am come that they might have life, and that more abundantly*.

With this simple concept as our clue, we can gain much insight by looking at nature herself. Throughout all of nature we see life striving for expression, seeking constantly for improvement of form and being through the process of evolution. If we can sense a purpose in nature, it must be simply the expression of life. But this brings us smack up against the next logical question: What is the *purpose* of life? If we can understand the purpose of life in its general sense, perhaps there will be the answer to the meaning of our individual existence.

What distinguishes a living organism from a blob of dead matter like a rock or a clod of dirt? We might say the ability to reproduce its own kind, or the method by which it derives nourishment from its environment. But the truly significant feature of life is *consciousness*. Some degree of consciousness is exhibited by every living organism from the single-celled amoeba through the plants and lower animals to its highest earthly form in man. When viewed from this standpoint, the whole process of evolution is obviously aimed at producing ever-higher forms of consciousness.

It is as if the Infinite Consciousness which created the universe is seeking to duplicate its infinity of consciousness on the plane of the particular. Therefore, we can reasonably equate consciousness to *livingness*. But this brings us to the simple conclusion that the purpose of life is to express more and more of itself in ever-upward spiraling approximation of the infinitude of the Creator. You may ask if there is any practical application to this bit of speculation. Yes! It can lead us to a useful understanding of our individual reason for living.

Your place in the scheme of things

In order to find our individual place in the scheme of the universe, it is necessary to dig a little deeper into the details of the great pattern. We have agreed that the expressed purpose of life is continual development of higher and higher forms of consciousness through the evolutionary process. But just how does that work?

Within each species, the law of natural selection works for the constant improvement of the type. This is also called the survival of the fittest, and it means exactly that. Only the stronger and more intelligent members of a species survive and thus have the opportunity to reproduce the kind. Thus the basic weaknesses are gradually weeded out of a species simply by the expedient death of those who have them. Throughout the world of nature we see how careful the great mother is of each species, but how unconcerned she is about the individuals within it. All the so-called laws of chance serve to perpetuate and improve the species at the expense of the inferior individuals.

The lower animals, lacking the precious gift of self-consciousness, don't understand this hard fact of nature, and so go on being chewed up by the laws of chance. This is also the case with most individual humans. They live from day to day subject to the unmerciful caprice of accidents, microbes, disease, pestilence, and the like, living, suffering, and dying with little thought to the reasons behind it all. It's a terrible waste for man to believe himself subject to these ancient laws! The first key to freedom lies in our objective consciousness, the ability to understand our relationship to our environment and to the Creator.

Now if the purpose of life is evolution, and the pattern for the lower species is chance, we are bound by the same laws until we figure a way out. But there is a way out! It lies in using our objective consciousness to establish a new relationship with the principles of evolution, based on our exercise of the *power to choose and cooperate.* The consciousness of *one* individual human being is sufficiently developed that it may realize and claim the same care from the forces of nature that is lavished on a whole species of lower creatures. *You can decide* that the old laws of chance will be replaced as they apply to your personal existence with a new set of laws which we might call the *laws of conscious cooperation with the evolutionary force.*

This understanding led the psalmist of old to exclaim, *What is man, that thou art mindful of him? And the son of man, that thou visitest him? For thou hast made him a little lower than the angels, and hast crowned him with glory and honour. Thou madest him to have dominion over the works of thy hands; thou hast put all things under his feet . . .* (Psalm 8:5)

Make your own decision to cooperate with the great forces of evolution! Then go to your quiet place and announce it to your spirit teachers. Send out your call to your spirit band; then in the silence say aloud something like this, "Beloved teachers, I am happy to tell you that I earnestly want to cooperate with the great evolutionary plan of the universe. I realize that I have much to learn, but even that is part of working for my own evolution. I pledge my best efforts henceforth to the accomplishment of my personal evolution and the maximum contribution to the upliftment and progress of all mankind. I will seek your special guidance in a quiet moment at least twice a day, and be alert at all times to your impressions of inspiration and help. I accept the tender, loving protection of all emissaries of God in whatever form they come, and proffer my wholehearted cooperation."

Then set out to discover your personal mission or reason for this particular incarnation, and fulfill it to the best of your ability.

How to discover your individual mission in this life

All of life is like a great symphony; and we, as individual expressions, are like the notes that combine to make the whole composition, complete with melody, harmony, counterpoint, and all the glorious details. When the orchestra is assembled to play, if just one note is omitted or comes out of sequence, the whole performance is something less than it might be. *Your individual contribution* is important to the great symphony we call life. And it is a fact that you agreed to achieve certain definite goals before you entered the tiny body that has grown up to be what the world considers you.

You are necessary for a special contribution to the progress of mankind during your lifetime. Isn't it about time you set out to discover what it is? There is a *wonderfully reciprocal relationship here:* Your own spiritual progress is advanced most by your special contribution to mankind's upward march. So how will you look for your mission?

Your first step is a careful review of the subconscious pattern of your past to get a look at the direction in which you have been led. Your subconscious is aware of the needs of your mission and has been working throughout your life to prepare you. Even your most glaring weaknesses were designed to assist in your grooming for the culmination of a lifetime of devotion to the progress of mankind. Some missions may seem bigger or more important than others, but that is only the appearance to our egocentric lower selves. In any symphony, some notes may stand out more than others, but all are necessary to the perfect whole.

We may gain an important insight by contemplating a story from the life of the Buddha. It is said that after six years of seeking enlightenment through the ascetic path, the young prince Gautama sat near a garden on the verge of death from his long starvation. A woman appeared bearing an offering of thanksgiving for the birth of her son and, mistaking Gautama for the wood god, fed him with the precious offering prepared from the milk of one hundred newly calved cows, which was fed to fifty white cows, whose milk was fed to twenty-five, and with theirs twelve more, and again with theirs to the six best of the herd, and that yield was boiled with fine spices and finely ground rice planted and individually picked with a pure heart. The purity of the nourishment so rejuvenated the young prince that he arose and proceeded to the Bodhi tree where his meditations brought on the enlightenment which made him the Buddha. Without those simple ministrations of the grateful mother, the world might well have been deprived of one of its greatest teachers.

Some of us have tasks to accomplish that may stand out like those of the Buddha, but most of us will find our lot to be more like that of the grateful mother. But each person's mission is well suited to his talents and experience, *and it is important to the overall progress of mankind.* The process of evolution, like its tool, the process of physical growth, is a steady heaping of many, many small achievements.

As you carefully review the subconscious pattern of your past life, pay attention to your problems as well as your special aptitudes and experience. Quiet meditation on the patterns you have discovered and prayerful consultation with your spiritual teachers will begin to reveal the general outlines of your mission. It is not necessary that you know the exact details until the time draws near for its fulfillment, and no amount of impatience will get the knowledge for you. Consider it enough to realize the broad outlines of your daily preparations, and strive to improve your effectiveness and your channels of communication with your spirit teachers whose guidance will be invaluable when it becomes your turn to take positive action. Work with them towards the time when you are meant to achieve.

How to direct your efforts toward accomplishing your spiritual mission

What is the best way to set about accomplishing your mission? First and most important, *maintain your balance* and continue to lead a normal life. The Oriental religions teach that life is divided into three major epochs which we might call childhood, the householder stage, and the later life when the family has been raised and there is more time and energy left for cultural and religious pursuits. It is important that we don't shirk our material responsibilities. How could you expect to stand in the presence of the Master and ask to join in service to mankind if you have not even fulfilled your regular obligations as a householder? That would be obviously absurd! We can take a lesson from the approach to the material world expounded by our Hindu and Buddhist friends. They tell us to *kill out all ambition for material advancement,* then *work as one who has it.*

Sounds shocking at first, doesn't it? But a little reflection will show you that here is the best way to succeed in the material world; without ambitious emotional involvement in your progress to cloud your thinking, you will naturally do a better job and get ahead faster. The by-product is an absence of guilt arising out of petty little plots to get ahead or yielding to temptations for unethical practices. Thus you can enter your twice daily meditation periods with a clear and untroubled mind, and progress unimpeded along the path of spiritual growth.

It is during your meditation periods that you should properly turn your attention to receiving guidance as to your spiritual mission and the means of accomplishing it. Your ever-improving relaxed awareness will reveal each opportunity for spiritual service as the time is right. Pay attention, but *keep your balance.* Nothing is as destructive of good spirit contact as anxiety. Be willing to take one simple step at a time, without always knowing what the next will be. Keep your faith and enjoy being a spectator as much as a participant in the unfoldment of your earthly sojourn.

Dr. George Washington Carver regularly talked with his "dear Creator" in the silence. His loving attention to the peanut, the flowers, and the clays of the soil in his "dear Creator's" presence brought forth such a multitude of new and

useful products that he revolutionized the entire economy of
the South. The depth of his personal faith shone so brightly
that it profoundly influenced the spiritual lives of countless
thousands. If he were standing before you now, his words
would tell you that any man can accomplish truly wonderful
works if he has enough love in his heart for his fellow man
and his "dear Creator." Let your love shine out through all
your actions as you strive toward the accomplishment of your
mission.

How to start your spiritual chain reaction of good

There is a great deal of truth to the old adage, "The Lord helps
him who helps himself." Spirit works most effectively by
amplifying the efforts of a human agency. Ask for guidance,
then *act on it* to the best of your ability, always keeping a
strong faith that help will be there whenever you need it. As
you learn to work more effectively, spirit will increase the
level of its help. It is rather like canasta or a paratroop invasion—the most successful people get the most help. Start your
own spiritual chain reaction of good, now! Go into your quiet
place and ask your teachers for instruction. Then act on the
impressions you receive. It can be the turning point of your
whole life.

A middle-aged woman was impressed by her teachers to
seek a class in psychic unfoldment. Her children were grown
now, so there was no question of lack of available time. She
made a few phone calls and the same class was recommended by several friends. Her progress seemed painfully slow at
first, but after six months she suddenly unfolded a wonderfully accurate ability to bring through messages from those now
living on the spirit side of life. She has since served thousands
of people, bringing many little personal proofs of survival of
individuality after the change people call death. The passing of
her husband left a physical void, but her ability to communi-

cate with him in her own quiet place considerably lessened her loneliness. She was able to live an economically productive later life by providing private readings for many seekers of truth.

A young man was finishing his second year of college, still with no idea of what he wanted for a career. Late one evening in his quiet place he saw a very clear symbol of himself in hospital garb performing an operation. A review of his first two years' classes showed he had been taking an excellent premedical course. He gave thanks for the previous subconscious guidance and threw himself into the study of medicine with a zeal born of the wonderful feeling of spirit cooperation. He is an excellent and highly successful surgeon today.

Your life can be enriched by *unfailing help* from on high! Seek your guidance, then start to help yourself. His angels will go before you, making your way happier and more productive than you dare even dream. Now is the best time to start!

Your path to peace of mind

Many people subscribe to the fallacy that contentment is the measure of peace of mind, but this tends to deflect their striving into less spiritually productive avenues. Peace of mind is a dynamic product of *achievement* that knows it can *and will* continually do better. Discontent can be an excellent tool of the spirit world in guiding us along our individual pathways of growth. We should always give thanks for our healthy discontent as a precious spiritual gift. It is the expression of our subconscious desires to work toward the fulfillment of our spiritual mission. You are assured of ever-increasing peace of mind if you train yourself to regularly view your discontent in these terms. Ask each little feeling of restlessness to reveal its spiritual message. Then pay attention to the answer—it will tell you more about your mission in life.

Progress in any field of endeavor is a direct result of somebody being dissatisfied with the status quo. In modern religious parlance, the driving force behind the advance of mankind is divine discontent. It is spirit urging us onward! By cooperating with the directing forces of spirit, you can turn each apparently negative emotion into a stepping stone to glorious growth for yourself and others. Ask each uncomfortable feeling for its spiritual message, then respond to your teacher's direction. As you regularly respond to the promptings of spirit, your life becomes a panorama of joyous progression. This is the true source of all personal peace.

Henry Ford's discontent with the transportation of the day led to the first mass production of the automobile, and changed our economy forever. Whitney's cotton gin, Douglas's airplane, and Land's Polaroid camera are similar examples of applied discontent. Each brought new comfort and happiness to many people.

Don't be afraid to think big, but don't refuse to take the small steps either. A mother was uneasy about the lack of crosswalks for children on the way to a nearby school. Her perseverance gathered enough signatures on a petition to get a city survey, which resulted in boulevard stop signs and a crossing guard during school hours. Who can tell how many young bodies were saved from harm by her efforts? Every step that helps others must help you. Start now!

POINTS TO REMEMBER

   I. Nature's purpose is the expression and improvement of life through the process of evolution.

  II. Life's purpose is to express evermore of itself, and thus the infinitude of the Creator.

 III. The laws of chance serve to improve the species at the expense of its inferior individuals.

  IV. You can lift yourself above the laws of chance by conscious cooperation with the forces of evolution.

    V. Seek to discover your personal mission in this life—your planned contribution to the progress of mankind.

    VI. To gain control of your progress: Kill out all ambition, then work as one who has it.

    VII. Spirit speaks to you of your mission through the avenue of divine discontent.

    VIII. Peace of mind is a dynamic product of achievement.

how
E.S.P. Can Insure
the Success of Your
Every Undertaking

It is the spirit that quickeneth; the flesh profiteth nothing: the words that I speak unto you, they are spirit and they are life. (John 7:63) As you learn to use your E.S.P. to stay in contact with spirit, your own life will be "quenched." You will find that the success of any undertaking is directly affected by its relationship to your spiritual mission. It is so certain that we can express it as a natural law.

The law of personal success

We can safely state that none of us is a Master, or we wouldn't need to be spending our time in this earthly classroom. Therefore, our own efforts are never enough to insure the success of our undertaking. *Spirit help is our key to success!* But your spirit teachers are not particularly interested in your worldly or material success. They hover near to assist in your personal growth and to see that you accomplish the tasks you accepted before you voluntarily entered the present earth life.

In this respect, worldly life is like a swiftly flowing stream. Any fool can float downstream with little or no effort simply by clinging to a passing log or piece of debris. But to go upstream, you need a boat with a powerful motor. The power for any upstream accomplishment must come from spirit, and this leads us to infer our law of personal success: *Any undertaking which prepares you for, or contributes to, your spiritual mission will succeed; and any undertaking which is incompatible with your spiritual mission will fail.*

You can avoid costly mistakes and failures by checking out each potential endeavor with your spirit teachers *before* you decide to try it. A successful corporate executive found an excellent opportunity to help a friend go into business for himself. Their special aptitudes were complementary, and the executive's contributions of time could be in his hobby hours, so he rushed into the deal without bothering to check with his spirit teachers. The enterprise was well planned and got off to a rousing good start. It made a profit the very first month, and after four months success seemed assured. But suddenly the executive discovered that his friend had been systematically diverting collections on account into his own pocket instead of into the business. In the legal battle that ensued, the business was ruined. Net result: The executive lost $10,000, five months of hard work moonlighting, and what he had thought was a good friend.

A somewhat belated meditation in his quiet place revealed the reason for his setback. The time he spent working in the sideline business was needed for him to begin writing a short self-help course in practical metaphysics. So six months late and $10,000 short, he began a successful metaphysical writing career in his hobby time. Spirit couldn't care less that he lost the money—it was a good spiritual lesson for him, and as soon as he got back on the spiritual track, prosperity again flowed to him in waves of abundance.

Another executive regularly paid more attention to his spirit teachers. One evening as he reached out to spirit in his quiet place, a strange light appeared on the wall. It formed itself into letters which said, "In three months the parent company will close your division with very little warning. Start discreetly sending out résumés as soon as possible, and we will help you relocate painlessly."

It came as quite a shock because he was happy with his position and knew that he was doing a good job in every way the situation allowed. But you don't argue with spirit when you receive such positive advice, so he followed directions. On the same day he was informed that the division would be closed, he received an offer of a new position with a local company at a slight increase in salary. By following directions, he was not jobless for even one day, and he avoided the anguish that naturally accompanies the unexpected closing of a material door.

The advantages of working with the spirit world are tremendously greater than anyone who hasn't experienced it can imagine. Let's look further into your part of working with spirit on new ideas.

How to examine a contemplated new undertaking in light of your spiritual mission

You were given a mind as one of the tools to be used during this earth life experience, and this is a good place to exercise it. Why bother spirit with questions about undertakings that common sense will tell you not to start? It should be obvious that anything you do must be honest and should not be harmful to others. Certainly it should be compatible with the spiritual view of life. If it fails to pass these simple ground rule tests, drop it at once!

If your idea passes the general ground rule tests, you are not yet ready to take it to spirit. You also need to pass a set of specific personal rules. Let's put them in the form of simple questions:

1. Does it provide new uses for many of your already developed aptitudes and strengths?
2. Will it provide opportunities to develop new strengths?
3. How would you feel about it in the awesome presence of your Maker?

If you can give positive answers to all three questions, you are at last ready to take it into meditation in your quiet place. Call for the presence of your spirit teachers and carefully explain your idea to them. Then *ask if it is compatible with your spirit mission.* Be careful that your anxiety and/or enthusiasm doesn't close your mind to spirit advice, and *wait for the answer.* It will always come. Feel it before you leave your quiet place!

As a simple example let's say you are thinking about taking a course in evening school. This is certainly honest and harmless, and advancement of personal knowledge is always compatible with the spiritual view of life. How about the personal tests? You would not be allowed to take the course if you had not fulfilled the prerequisites, so we can assume it will provide new uses for your present strengths; and its whole purpose is to provide opportunity to develop new strengths, skills, or knowledge. I can think of no course offered by a socially responsible educational institution that might cause you to feel uncomfortable in the presence of the Creator. It has now passed all the mental tests, and as far as you can logically tell, it should be a good move for you. Now you are ready to take it before your spirit teachers for their special counsel. Go to your quiet place, relax, and call for your teachers. Tell them, "I am considering taking this particular course in night school and it seems like a good thing for me to do. Please give me the benefit of your wider vision. Will it fit into my spiritual mission?" In the ensuing silence one may be impressed, "It is good for you, little sister, do not hesitate!" Another may hear, "Not this year, my brother, it would be too great a strain on your health." And yet another might suddenly feel, "It would be good for you, but there is something much better just over the horizon. You would be wiser to wait for it."

When you ask in this manner, your teachers will consistently give you sound advice, but it is important to realize that the *decision is always your own.* It is your personal responsibility to decide and act in your own life! This can never be delegated or abdicated. It is analogous to consulting an expert on Earth. You may go to your attorney with a legal problem and receive sound advice as to your alternatives and their probable outcomes; but the decision and the responsibility remain forever your own. The more you think and act responsibly, the greater help you will naturally draw from the spirit world. It is another working of the law of natural selection—*them that has, gets.*

Coming out of the armed services just after World War II, a man was pondering his choice of two proffered positions. One appeared to offer better opportunity for advancement, while the other offered a better starting salary. Certainly he needed to work for a living, so the ground rule questions were satisfied. He decided to take both offers into his quiet place and consult his spirit teachers. In the silence he received an unexpected answer: "You are leaning toward the position that seems to offer the best chance of future progress, and that is laudable. But there is a setback coming to that company within the year, and it will keep the occupant of your potential position tied down for several years. Take the job that pays more money, and apply yourself. You will be pleased with your progress."

By listening to the voice of spirit, the man avoided a material setback and launched a highly successful career. The same good guidance is yours if you will but ask, *and listen!*

How to summon your spirit teachers to assist you

When you reach the point in your meditation where you know spirit agrees your undertaking is in keeping with your basic mission, rejoice! You can be sure, now, that your teachers are ready and eager to help you. But they can do little without your specific permission for them to help.

Don't be the "Please, mother, I'd rather do it myself" type. Ask for spirit help. Your teachers are real people, and you will get the best results if you treat them that way. Talk to them just as you would talk to a good friend who still inhabits an earthly body. You have attracted your special set of spirit teachers because you all share in the same basic mission. They are literally partners in your progress, so your success is theirs also. They will help you in countless ways, but they won't do the things you can and should do for yourself. Again remember that spirit works best by *amplifying your efforts.* So put out some effort for your friends to amplify.

A young man working at the very bottom in a furniture factory began to get an urge for a career in electronics. He took this feeling to his teachers in his quiet place and asked for guidance. In the peaceful atmosphere of the meditation, everything seemed to make sense, so he enrolled in an electronic assembly class at night. After twelve weeks of hard work he received a certificate and began his search for a suitable job. He was chosen over fourteen other applicants with similar backgrounds for his first job in electronic assembly. Next came the urge for an engineering degree, and again he sought guidance in his quiet place. This time help came in the form of his company's financing the cost of books and tuition in the evening at a local college. It took eight years of hard work, but he regularly advanced on the job as the new educational work improved his qualifications, and his years in the shop contributed to his being one of the top electronic production engineers in the state.

A middle-aged man was told that his wife needed a very serious operation. They were both working, and it seemed to take all they could earn to keep the children in high school and make ends meet. In his quiet place he talked over his intense desire to find a way to finance the operation. After he covered all the details, he sat in the silence and waited. After about ten minutes a voice seemed to say, "Worry not, good brother, you will have help within three days."

On the third day there was a check for $2,000 in the mailbox together with a letter from an attorney in a distant state explaining that this was a bequest from the estate of a distant uncle.

Regularly call on your spirit teachers for help, then cooperate! *Help will be there whenever you need it.*

Your law of growth

We have regularly alluded to the price of all this spirit help as your striving to align yourself with the goals of your personal spiritual mission. Regardless of what direction that might lead to, your personal growth is the best possible catalyst for its accomplishment. Look around you at the lower animal and the plant kingdoms; the lower a species in the evolutionary scheme of things, the more certainly its individuals lack the choice of their activities. For instance, dogs and monkeys move about freely, but trees and shrubs are restricted to one location for a whole lifetime. But the *one major requirement* of *all* individuals of *all* species is *personal growth.*

The law of life is growth, and its opposite is stagnation or decay. Everywhere you turn, you see evidence of vigorous growth or signs of decay. *Nothing ever stands still!* The law of nature is to *grow* or to *die* and make room for the new growth of something else. It matters not if your chronological age is 20, 60, or 99 years; your choice is still the same: Grow or die! Because we humans are blessed with the most comprehensive mental faculties, it falls upon us to take a greater initiative in directing and perpetuating our personal growth processes.

Yes, I believe you can grow a new hand or foot if you need it! But if you are blessed with a complete and well-functioning physical "horse" to ride through life, it is all the more important not to relax your striving. We began the first chapter with simple exercises for psychic and spiritual growth, and everything that has come since is pointed in the same direction. What are your personal weaknesses? You can grow by consciously working to improve each weak area, be it physical, mental, financial, psychic, or spiritual. Most intelligent people would want to do that anyway. But by itself this is not enough! Your true fulfillment will come as you strive to exploit your strengths in the direction of accomplishing that part of your mission which is most obvious to you now.

A young man in a junior supervisory position began to feel the stirring of an urge deep within his being. It kept saying, "Perhaps you were meant to be a minister." For a long time he contented this urge by reading books on comparative religions and metaphysics. Then he subscribed to several *New Thought* publications and started to take courses in metaphysics. His embryonic attempts at application of the principles he studied brought advancement on his job and added new meaning to his daily existence. More and more he felt he must definitely contribute to mankind's progress in these broad fields. As time passed he became increasingly successful in his material work with personal earnings near the top 10 percent of individuals in the nation, but he was still stirred by the urge to serve in a religious capacity. In his late fifties, he began courses in the "development of mediumship" and gradually unfolded an excellent ability in that field. It was not until he reached what most people call the retirement age that he found himself in a position to serve with his new ability. All the later years of his very productive life were brightened by the joy of serving as a medium for messages from the spirit world. He would be the first to agree that his material success was tremendously aided by his lifelong preparation for that vague spiritual goal.

Your spiritual mission may not be scheduled for accomplishment tomorrow or next week, but your earnest seeking and preparation will certainly benefit every area of your present life. Follow that urge to learn something new! Every talent you develop will contribute to your progress and to that of mankind as a whole.

How to succeed every time

Some men seem to succeed in everything they try, while others crawl along over the carcasses of their many failures. *Success is never an accident!* It may look easy for some, but it is always a result of carefully laid spiritual groundwork. We might describe the secret of success by a simple three-step formula:

1. Unify with your spiritual mission.
2. Summon your subconscious and spirit help.
3. Let your success grow and *work* to make it even better.

Whatever you undertake must be compatible with your spiritual mission to insure success. Screen each desire carefully, and take the worthy ones into your quiet place for spirit help in determining their compatibility. When you get the spiritual green light, ask for help from your subconscious realms and from your personal spirit helpers. Renew your spirit contact twice daily in your quiet place and ask for help each time, never forgetting to give thanks for the help you have already received. Then make your physical start and give spirit plenty of your own effort to amplify on behalf of your success. Keep faith in your spirit teachers and they will never forsake you. Success in any endeavor is yours for the spiritual trying.

Walter Russell combined his concentrated desire with a deep abiding faith in God to become successful in music, literature, architecture, painting, sculpture, and philosophy. He attributed his success to his unity with the "Universal One" and to his belief that he *must* do each thing as it presented itself, and he *should* do it as a demonstration of his belief in man's unlimited power. He left us the challenge that communion between the self and the "Universal Self" is the only way to achieve the impossible.

With God, all things are possible. Tune in on the spiritual success wavelength, now!

POINTS TO REMEMBER

I. The law of personal success: Any undertaking which prepares you for, or contributes to, your spiritual mission will succeed; and any undertaking which is incompatible with your spiritual mission will fail.

II. Use your common sense in evaluating potential new ventures.

III. Specific rules for spirit help:

    A. Does it provide new uses for many of your already developed aptitudes and strengths?

    B. Will it provide opportunities to develop new strengths?

    C. How would you feel about it in the presence of your Maker?

IV. Ask your teachers if it is compatible with your spiritual mission.

 V. The law of growth: Grow or die!

VI. The three steps to success:

    A. Unify with your spiritual mission.

    B. Summon your subconscious and spirit help.

    C. Let it grow, and *work* to make it better.

how to
Use E.S.P. to Establish a Personal Relationship with God

As you improve your contact and learn to work with your spirit teachers, you will quite naturally feel a closer relationship to the great life force of the universe that people call God. Certainly no one in communication with the other side of life would deny its existence. But there is a much deeper, personal experience of God that longs to manifest for you. Down through the ages, spiritual people of all faiths have experienced momentary periods of communion with God in a personal way, beyond time and space. Religionists generally call this the "mystic" experience, Freud called it the "oceanic feeling," and Jesus called it the "pearl of great price." Regardless of the name you choose to hang on it, we can agree that this is the most important single experience in any person's life. Let's begin a systematic search for your personal experience, now.

How your active intuition expands your concept of God

Primitive men of all ages recognize a whole host of gods: a god of the river, of the wind, the hunt, the sunshine, the rain, the tree, the rock, and on and on. By looking at the personalities projected upon their gods by these backward believers, we can get a better understanding of our own concepts. And what are the principal characteristics? The gods are all more powerful than man, but they demonstrate very human emotions and weaknesses. The regular practice of the primitive is the attempt to flatter or bribe the gods with praise and sacrifices in order to seek favor or ward off wrath.

An interesting remnant of this old process is the rain dance of the American Indian by which the spirit of rain is propitiated ~appease and drought is brought to an end. Similarly, it is normal in some (pacify) primitive cultures to bring a gift to the river god to bribe his favor for a safe crossing. We may snicker at such practices in the smugness of our modern society, but in a larger sense we haven't come so very far from those things ourselves.

We claim to worship one living God, but what is our concept of Him? The Old Testament is full of descriptions of the anger and vindictiveness of the Hebrew idea of God. For instance: *And they forsook the Lord, and served Baal and Ashtaroth. And the anger of the Lord was hot against Israel and he delivered them into the hands of their enemies round about, so that they could not any longer stand before their enemies.* (2 Judges 2:13, 14)

Have we really come so far from that concept? Isn't this the basis of what our psychologist friends call subconscious guilt? Fortunately for the collective psyche of the whole Western world, there entered upon the scene a man of great stature whose mission was to emphasize that our God is a God of love. For those who can simply accept the concept of vicarious atonement, Jesus of Nazareth brought the perfect gift of freedom from guilt. After all, if the Master gave His earthly life on the cross for the forgiveness of your sins, what have you to be guilty about?

This was a simple teaching for the primitive mass mind of its day, and it is harder to swallow by today's intellectual standards. The modern thinking man finds it just as hard to accept the dogma of original sin as vicarious atonement, and that is good for him. Thus he is in a position to make his own peace with the Universal Life Force, but only if he can free himself from the haunting subconscious doubts and guilts of yesteryear. It is good for our wavering subconscious to be treated with some of Jesus' teachings of love and law to offset the collective sense of guilt that impinges upon us in unguarded moments:

These things have I spoken unto you, that my joy might remain in you, and that your joy might be full. This is my commandment, That ye love one another, as I have loved you. Greater love hath no man than this, that a man lay down his life for his friends. (John 15:11-13) Some meditation on this in your own quiet place will help prepare your subconscious for its part in your coming experience. The basic idea is to get more and more love attached to your concept of God. We have chosen these words of Jesus because they are the prelude to our understanding of that often misconstrued statement: . . . *he that hath seen me hath seen the Father* . . . (John 14:9)

Obviously Jesus wasn't referring to his *physical body* as the *me* which when seen is to see the Father. We must make a distinction in our thinking between the man, Jesus, and the Christ Spirit which manifested through Him. Our best translation of the quotation would probably be, "He who has seen the pure love of the Christ Spirit manifesting through me has seen the Father."

You can never reach God through your intellect. In a larger sense you can never reach God at all—that is, without a gift from on high which the orthodox Christians most often call *grace*. The mystic experience is indeed a gift from God Himself, but you must first be prepared to receive it. The beginning of preparation is to expand your concept of God. This is a job for your intuition. Spend a little time in your quiet place daily, for as long as necessary, meditating on your highest concept of God. Let your intuition explore the depths of the infinite love which created the beauty of life and the vastness of the universe, and yet has a tremendous individualized love for something as tiny as you. Grow yourself a wonderful new, living concept of the infinite, loving God.

The reciprocal relationship among you, your spirit teachers, and God

A closer look at your spirit teachers will help your expanding concept of God. Truly, He has given His angels charge over you, and they do keep you in all of your ways. But just who and what are they? All of them have had bodies of earthly flesh and have experienced the strange mixture of suffering and joy that we call life on Earth. Many of them will have new earthly bodies one of these days, and the accomplishments they help you attain here and now will certainly help them then. Where are they? What are they? In the *Bhagavad-Gita* the Lord, Krishna, explains to Arjuna: When a man *dies* he first goes to the exact heaven of his own belief. Then after a stay of an appropriate time, the soul enters again into the scheme of things on the other side of life while preparing for a new birth into a brand new earthly body.

Whether or not you agree with the two-thirds of the world's population who believe in reincarnation, you can accept the simple fact that your spirit teachers once had bodies of flesh, but now have been relieved of the confines and demands of their mortal bodies. Therefore, they have no requirement to earn a living in the same sense as we who remain on Earth; and the absence of the demands of the flesh gives them the opportunity for much clearer spiritual vision, and in some cases even the ability to predict selected future events on Earth. Yet, one who has passed over prematurely will feel a tremendous handicap in trying to complete the projects he left undone.

Plainly, the better communications you establish with your spirit teachers, the better you will be able to learn from them and profit by their guidance. Always remember that you attract the kind of spirits which more completely blend with your personality and approach to life. If you should receive a suggestion that you do someone physical or psychological harm or commit a criminal act, break off communications at once and begin praying for the blessing of light to come to the offending spirit. Such occurrences should be extremely rare in the experience of any spiritually oriented person, but we all have negative periods during which we might attract a spirit of lesser evolvement. This is simply a word of caution. No spirit of the light would advise you to hurt another person or commit anything resembling a crime! *You are always responsible for your own actions,* regardless of whose advice you are taking.

Now back to the good part. Use your ever-growing rapport with your teachers to help expand your concept of God. You can talk to them about God and receive many uplifting impressions and ideas. When you enter your quiet place to meditate on your growing relationship with God, invite your teachers to be present and to participate. The beautiful part about spiritual work is that there is no competition. There will be no jealousy on the part of your teachers, and absolutely no feeling that you are trying to go over their heads. Everything that helps your personal progress also helps them, and from their spiritual vantage point they are totally aware of it. Best of all they are able to feed you new ideas on the fringes of your current understanding, thus helping you grow into a richer, fuller relationship with God. There is a deeply personal experience and relationship to be gained! Seek it either through the intercession of your teachers, or directly by your own efforts. But *seek* it!

How to reach God through your spirit teachers

In the modern Catholic Church it is considered normal and even necessary to pray for help to the Saints of the Church. But who are the Saints? They are people who led such exemplary lives while in the flesh that some time after their passing they were, in effect, voted into sainthood by the Church Fathers. Thus we can postulate that one of the great foundations of the Catholic Church is *spiritual contact* in the form of prayer to the Saints and answers received by those who pray. This is not too different from Oriental ancestor worship which also involves spirit contact. In the *Bhagavad-Gita,* Krishna himself gives the mystic experience to Arjuna; and in most forms of yoga the master works with the student to assist in his achievement of the same result.

Thus it is not only reasonable, but also nearly universal to ask for individual spirit help as one truly aspires to the depth of mystic experience. When your meditations have unfolded much of the vast subliminal–intuitive area of relationship to the Living God, you are ready to ask for help. Ask always, call on your teachers and talk it over with them. They are your best friends as well as your most effective helpers. Ask for their guidance in your preparations to receive the mystic experience, and for their specific help in attaining it. Your own relaxed awareness is your best contribution to the cooperative accomplishment. Pay careful attention to the guidance and direction, and *follow it.*

How Gladys G. found enrichment

For years Gladys G. had been pushed by a vague but persistent inner spiritual longing. She investigated several "mystery schools," belonged to several "new age" churches, and had finally unfolded a good measure of E.S.P. It seemed that each new bit of progress only whetted her appetite for much more. Her husband was patient with her search because she had always been a loving and good wife. One day he was inspired to ask her a startling question: "Why don't you use this E.S.P. of yours to ask some spiritual being what it is that seems to be gnawing at you?"

Recognizing this as a wonderful piece of spiritual advice, she took the question into her quiet place for meditation. The first time she asked there was no answer because she had become so anxious and excited that she couldn't receive anything but spiritual static. She worked at relaxing, and by the third morning she reached a degree of serenity that could not be denied. In an intuitive flash came the answer: "You seek a deeply personal relationship with God." Naturally her immediate question was, "How shall I go about attaining such a wonderful gift?" And again came that flash: "Your own spirit teachers will help you tomorrow morning. Arrange an uninterrupted hour and begin it in meditation. You will be directed and assisted by the highest help we can summon."

This time Gladys knew better than to go in excitement or tension. She spent the evening in attentive care of her husband and managed to stay relaxed enough to get a good night's sleep. Next morning she approached her quiet place with relaxed but happy anticipation. She called on her teachers and waited in silence. Shortly she was impressed to lie down on the bed. Following directions without question, she complied and soon was comfortably relaxing in the horizontal position. In a few minutes she fell into a light trance and was treated to an out-of-body experience she could find no words to describe. Suffice it to say that her life was enriched and given new meaning and purpose from an inner certainty that is unshakable.

This gift can be yours also. Seek it!

How to reach God directly

For those who were raised in the Protestant faith, it is encouraging to know that the mystic experience can be yours directly and without your conscious knowledge of help from the spirit world. Ever since Martin Luther introduced the *do it yourself* movement into Christianity, hardy souls have been seeking the *light* on their own. And seeking always pays off to those who are sincere.

Generally the first experience is spontaneous when it comes directly, and it comes as quite a surprise to its recipient. As an excellent example of this, I quote from a letter sent to me by a lady in the midwestern United States:

> One morning I had already risen for the day but something prompted me to flop across the foot of my bed and

sort of wake up more fully. And a strange sight came in view, like two diamond-shaped frames in which were enclosed sparkling jewels (not lights) like the glitter of precious stones. Some blinked off, others on—off and on they went, all colors for a few seconds, beautiful beyond description. Then they dimmed out and I saw sky and stars like the whole universe moving to the right and gradually fading out. Something within me made me reason, I'm seeing the whole Universe, but it neither excited me nor scared me.

I had an experience in the spring of 1952 that was the beginning of my earnest seeking in this field, and it may help your understanding to share it. It was my first out-of-body experience, and I found myself standing in utter darkness in the center of a huge dome-shaped structure. Suddenly a great shaft of light shone down from somewhere above, engulfing me. I felt that I was completely alone in this light when a voice spoke with great authority, "Let him whose eye is single lift himself up and reveal God."

Then a tremendous power surged through my being and I was able to levitate my body and float through the air with ease. This seemed to be the normal method of travel between various groups of people whom I addressed from a floating position about six feet above the ground. You can imagine my disappointment upon returning to my physical body and finding that these wonderful powers had not returned with me. This was the initial challenge to do something spiritually worthwhile with this life.

But we don't want to wait for some chance bit of *luck* to bring about our mystic experience. Let's get on with a program to bring it about for you. By now it should be deeply meaningful to you to contemplate the fact that *you are spirit. God is spirit and you are created in His image and likeness.* We have agreed that the self-contemplation of spirit is the original creative force. Since you are spirit, your contemplation of God is truly the self-contemplation of spirit, and as such must be itself creative. So the secret is to enter your quiet place and contemplate God. Imagine the richest personal relationship with God that your expanded concepts can encompass, and claim it as yours now. Thus, as spirit, you can truly create your own mystic experience.

Of course, it is necessary to surmount the same old stumbling blocks of doubt and fear. They will try to haunt you with questions like: Do you dare? Are you worthy? Isn't this all really just nonsense? If you are bothered by these doubts, read some Whitman, or Meister Eckhart, or Thomas Aquinas. The mystical writings of great men such as these will convince you that there is nothing more worthwhile than the mystic experience.

Then go into your quiet place and reach inside yourself to the infinity which is God. I want to share one more experience with you. It was a quiet Saturday afternoon, and I was stretched out on the couch contemplating these great truths. Suddenly I seemed to enter another realm of consciousness and I felt those great words of Psalm 91 spoken not as words, but as the law of the universe: *Because he hath set his love upon me, therefore will I deliver him: I will set him on high, because he hath known my name. He shall call upon me, and I will answer him: I will be with him in trouble; I will deliver him, and honour him. With long life will I satisfy him, and shew him my salvation.* Seek it! There is nothing beside it.

How your mystic experience will change your life forever

No amount of words spoken or written will ever take the place of your personal mystic experience. However you may imagine the splendor and wonder of it will prove incomplete by a whole dimension when you have the real thing to compare with it. It may last for a few moments or an hour, or it may come and go regularly. But your first glimpse will show you that *the light is real*. Something happens deep within your being, though it may seem to be happening outside somewhere. For the truth is that at that moment, you and the universe *are one* in a totality of feeling and realness that defies the limitations of the language. Suddenly you *know,* and you need no further proof. But what do you know? Even that defies description, but it includes your *ownership of eternal life,* your brotherhood with all living creatures, and your personal relationship with God. It is suddenly yours forever, and nobody can take it away from you!

Now it's time to get this experience into the proper perspective. Spirit used an interesting analogy to help me, and it seems worth passing along here. Think of yourself as a very young flying fish. You have lived all of your short life beneath the surface of the ocean in the relative darkness of the deep. This compares to the normal physical life we all lead on Earth. Now the wonderful day comes when you are attracted by the shimmering surface above. Instinctively you gather the necessary speed and make your first fantastic flight up into the sunshine and air above the water. For a few seconds you soar on your young wings, completely exhilarated by the new experience; but just as surely as you soared up there, you must shortly fall back into the great ocean. Your consciousness is forever changed, and you will seek to soar in the wonderful world above many times during your lifetime. But you cannot escape the fact that you are a fish. It will avail you nothing to bemoan the fate that has made you dependent for the life of your body upon the sustenance to be derived only from living under the water.

There is much to be learned from this little analogy. We have come to the classroom called earth life to learn and to grow. Some of us realize our potential as *flying fish* and manage to soar momentarily in the great mystical union with God and His Universe. But just as surely as we enter this wonderful experience, we are deposited once more into the same life, with its same mundane problems and the same seeming drudgery of routine living. Shall we be stupid and bemoan our fate? That could only hurt your progress. The wise man will give thanks on his knees for the momentary respite from the classroom of life. He may look upon this wonderful experience as recess and look forward to another with the same happy anticipation as a young schoolboy awaiting the recess of his class. But *this is not an excuse to abdicate our earthly responsibilities!*

Yes, your life is changed permanently. You can't help but be happier and more at ease for the rest of your life. But you created a set of earth problems that you must still work out, and you contracted to accomplish a mission before you entered the body of this incarnation. Your mystic experience shows that you are making wonderful spiritual progress. This is certainly not the time to fall by the wayside and waste your golden opportunity for service and growth. Give thanks for the infinite joy of the mystic experience, and seek it often, even as the flying fish often soars. But come back to Earth refreshed and willing to be an *effective part of society!* Live the practical mystic life.

How to live the practical mystic life

One of the great gifts of your mystic experience is a new frame of reference for all of life. You have a new feeling of oneness with all of God's creatures, so you will be much less inclined to hurt anything or anybody. Such sports as hunting and fishing lose much of their luster, and some mystics become vegetarians so as not to take their sustenance from the killing of sentient beings. There is a danger of going out of balance with such practices, and you should be careful of the effect on others if you carry your new inclinations to extreme. Having spent an interesting three years as a vegetarian myself, I can tell you for sure that you can be a double-barreled nuisance to your friends without half trying. A vegetarian is almost an impossible guest to nonvegetarians, and a bit of perspective will help you understand that it is all a matter of degree anyway.

Yes, it's good to live such a life that you bring a minimum of suffering to your fellow creatures. But science has shown that even a tomato registers anxiety or pain when cut with a knife, so why should we kick up a big fuss? The Creator in His infinite wisdom gave us bodies which require much of the protein and amino acids found in meat, and who are we to question Him? There are many carnivorous animals besides man, and we don't condemn them for living as their bodies were designed. So don't condemn yourself either! Live as normal a life as possible, and let your new light shine through to the many acts of kindness and friendship you find the opportunity to bestow upon your fellow creatures.

You should be a joy to all who meet you! Follow your happy impulses to kindness and generosity, but again a note of balance is in order. You may feel impelled to save the whole world, but your resources may temporarily limit you to simple and inexpensive acts of kindness. The tendency is to forget yourself completely, but this is as utterly ridiculous as complete selfishness. You are very like the goose that laid the golden egg. The goose must be fed and cared for if it is to continue to produce. Don't let some greedy imbecile kill it and cut off the supply for everyone.

Because of your mystic experience, you are now God's personal ambassador to mankind. Strive to follow the injunction of your *older brother* who came to show us the way: *Let your light so shine before men, that they may see your good works, and glorify your Father which is in heaven.* (Matt. 5:16) But it isn't prudent to run off looking for some personal cross to get tacked up on! The Master's sacrifice was intended to be enough to last mankind for all time. You are of more use to the world healthy and alive. Live to experience the true joy of helping others and of fulfilling your own spiritual mission. Your achievements will bless you into all of eternity.

Then let's be sure we understand that the mystic experience is not the ultimate achievement, either. It is indeed the most wonderful individual experience presently imaginable, but it should be considered more as a new beginning than as an end in itself. In one sense it is like the proverbial carrot held in front of the rabbit to induce him to pull the cart faster. Here is your taste of what true spiritual oneness with God can mean;

now come on back to Earth and *earn* the right to dwell there always. As you labor in His vineyards and strive to feed His sheep, you will unfold evermore of your inner spirituality until you learn to dwell in His secret place of the most high. *"He that dwelleth in the secret place of the most high shall abide under the shadow of the Almighty. I will say of the Lord, He is my refuge and my fortress: my God; in him will I trust. . . . He shall cover thee with his feathers [of love] and under his wings shalt thou trust. . . ."* These words are no longer just the poetic mouthings of an ancient shepherd boy, *they have shown themselves to be the law of your being.*

Enjoy your sojourn with the Creator and let it be the inspiration for your life of meaningful service to mankind.

POINTS TO REMEMBER

   I. Our doubts and guilts stand between us and our personal mystic experience.

  II. In meditation, let your intuition grow you a wonderfully new, living concept of the infinite, loving God.

 III. Ask your spirit teachers for help in achieving your mystic experience.

 IV. Seek it directly; claim your personal relationship with God.

  V. Your life will be changed forever but keep your balance!

how to
Use Advanced Psychic Phenomena for E.S.P.

You may have wondered why we stuck with just the very elementary and basic forms of E.S.P. throughout the first nine chapters. Even though there might be more glamour in some other approach, all educators agree that a sound groundwork of fundamentals is necessary before building the superstructure. My personal feeling is that the work of Chapter 9 is an absolute prerequisite to any intelligent excursion into advanced psychic phenomena. But we have worked for lo these nine chapters, now let's play! Let's have a go at the glamour part of E.S.P.

Now you are ready for advanced phenomena

The humility that comes from a deep mystical experience, or at least from a thorough understanding of the idea, gives you a sound appreciation of the next dimension. You can easily understand the simple confession of the Master, *When ye have lifted up the son of man, then shall ye know that I am he, and that I do nothing of myself; but as the Father taught me, I speak these things.* (John 8:28)

It is for lack of this humility that many areas of E.S.P. have accumulated what we might call a bit of a bad name. A few psychics and mediums seem to forget that it is not their little self which is doing the work, and the unfortunate result is jealousy, backbiting, and even fraudulent demonstrations. Happily these people are few in number, but the sincere workers have a great task in living down the negativity. However, we have long since ceased to condemn the whole medical profession for an occasional quack, and we must now do the same for the workers in E.S.P. If you feel impelled to do so, enter the work; but take care to bring your humility with you.

We are about to survey a vast panorama of fascinating psychic phenomena, but it is important that we pause for one more word of caution. The Master cautioned us, *Give not that which is holy unto the dogs, neither cast ye your pearls before swine, lest they trample them under their feet, and turn again and rend you.*

Psychic phenomena is for the use and instruction of seekers and believers, not for parlor games. Use sound spiritual judgment in choosing when and where to use it. Its misuse will set you back much further than you might think. From this somewhat sober mental platform, we will begin our happy exploration of the deeper psychic realms.

Types of experience you may expect

In a work of this size we can hardly scratch the surface of the wonderful world of the psychic, but we will begin with a brief description of some of the more common occurrences.

1. KNOCKS AND RAPS

Spirits often indicate their presence, or even enter into the conversation, with distinct knocks or raps on the wall, a window, or some piece of furniture. This simple manifestation is present in many places where it is ignored or shrugged off as *the house settling, the wind blowing,* or the like. I attended a gathering of people at a very nice lady's house. During an interesting bit of conversation about spiritual things, there came a loud rap on the wall indicating a visiting spirit's agreement with what was said. A little dog heard, and I believe saw, the spirit and barked a friendly greeting. I looked up and said, "Hi, there." But our hostess immediately said, "Oh, it's just the wind."

It is highly unfriendly to snub our spirit friends in such a manner. Yes, some creaks may be from strains on the structure of a house, but there are unquestionably others which are real manifestations from the spirit side of life. Pay just a little attention and you can easily tell the difference. I once had an end table in my living room that was made something like a box, open in front but closed on the back and sides. Every night around bedtime, one of our spirit friends told us "good night" by sounding three quick raps, one on each side and one on the back of this little end table. We enjoyed him immensely, but you would be amazed at the unnerving effect it had on some of our visiting earth friends. There is no reason to be frightened of this friendly manifestation from the spirit world. They will give you stronger raps if you get in the habit of saying "hello" to them.

2. AURA VISION

In the chapter on spiritual healing we discussed the human aura and its relation to the health of your body. As you work to develop your aura vision, you will begin to occasionally notice an aura that is not attached to a living human body. This is not a trick of your tired eyes! You are privileged to look at the aura of a visiting spirit entity. Again a friendly greeting will help the spirit to better manifest to you. Here is a wonderful chance to use your developing clairaudience or clairsentience to enter a more direct communication with the world of spirit.

We are often visited in our living room by such spirit manifestations. They remain anywhere from a minute or two to a couple of hours, and we often manage very interesting conversations. It's just as much fun to be visited by a spirit friend as by one who still has a body. Why not enjoy both? Nothing can help you achieve this more than your own relaxed awareness and a friendly attitude toward those gracious spirits who come visiting.

3. AUTOMATIC WRITING

Some well-meaning spiritualists will warn you of the dangers of automatic writing, but they are dangers only to the emotionally unbalanced. With your inner strength born of the mystic's understanding of the universe, there is nothing to fear at all. If you care to give it a try, it is best to set a regular time either once a day or once a week, and announce this to your spirit teachers. Then on your schedule, sit down in the comfortable place you have chosen, armed with pencil and paper. Relax for a moment and call on your spirit teachers for protection and assistance. Then ask if they have anyone who wishes to write through you. Next hold the pencil in your normal writing position on the paper and let spirit move your hand, causing it to write. It may take more than one sitting before anything happens, but almost everybody will get some results within a reasonable time.

It is when you start getting results that you need to keep your judgment and reason about you. You can often get real words of wisdom and good spiritual advice by this technique, but sometimes it is possible to contact a lesser evolved entity who will flatter you, lie to you, or even direct you to do something ridiculous or criminal. If the writing begins telling you that you are a great avatar or a reincarnation of Napoleon, or asks you to go shoot Joe Doaks down the street, break off the contact and ask your spirit teachers to assist the offending spirit to find light. Like most other spirit manifestations, this technique works very well for some, not so well for others, and not at all for those who tense up and refuse to let spirit move their hands. It is well worth a try for any spiritually oriented person.

4. INSPIRATIONAL WRITING

A useful variation of automatic writing / rational writing. Again you sit with pencil a on your teachers to be with you. Tell them that you are ready to write under their inspiration, then relax. Very soon you will be impressed with an idea. Write it down in your own words, and likely as not another will come to you while you are still writing the first. Whether consciously or not, most authors use this technique for virtually all of their writing.

Though I will certainly accept the responsibility for any errors which have crept in, I must confess that both this book and the earlier one, *The Miraculous Laws of Universal Dynamics,* were produced by inspirational writing. It is truly amazing how much you learn when you sit down to work for spirit through this medium. One teacher in particular handles a great deal of this work through me; I call him Professor Reinhardt. While handling some of the more difficult ideas, we will often seem to "write ourselves into a corner," and I instinctively stop and look up laughingly with the question, "O.K., Reinhardt, how are we going to get out of this one?"

Instantly there will come an intuitive flash that clearly shows it was me in the corner, not the spirit helper whose higher vision had it all planned from the beginning. Anyone who will take the trouble to develop some degree of sensitivity can become an effective messenger of spirit through this simple technique. Experiment with a little automatic writing first to get the feel of the thing, then try this. You will be glad you did.

5. INSPIRATIONAL LECTURING

Quite similar to inspirational writing is the phenomenon of inspirational lecturing. Certainly the whole world would agree that the best speakers don't simply read a previously written speech. They may use a set of notes to chart the course, but the real meat of the lecture comes through more or less spontaneously. I was privileged to attend regular Sunday lectures by one of the most powerful religious speakers in the country. His voice literally filled the large auditorium with guidance, inspiration, and a lively wit. Experiencing the man in this manner built a mental image of him as almost 10 feet tall and a virtual human dynamo. When I finally met him in the flesh, he turned out to be short (about 5 feet 5 inches) and mild mannered almost to the point of being retiring. But every time he walked out on that platform, he was transformed by the spiritual light and turned into a fantastic showman as well as an inspiration to all within earshot.

Not everyone gets the chance to speak before a group regularly, but it will be good for you to accept any and all invitations to do so. Prepare by calling on your spirit teachers for inspiration and specific help. Then choose your subject and make a short outline—stick to subjects that are familiar to you so you can keep your poise and confidence. When your turn comes, stand up and speak! The first three times are the hardest. After that it honestly gets to be fun, and you can bring much solid inspiration to many people. Never refuse an invitation! Your spirit teachers want to work through you.

6. PSYCHOMETRY

There is a vibratory essence in any object which picks up the happenings and moods of its surroundings and the people who handle it. With a little practice, you can hold someone's watch or ring and tell him how he feels today, what he has been thinking about, who gave him the object and under what circumstances, and countless little things that have occurred while he was wearing or carrying it.

This practice is called psychometry, and extensions of the technique are manifold in the psychic world. There is some argument as to whether the object merely forms a convenient point of concentration for reading the mental aura of the subject or actually carries the vibrations itself. Your mystical *knowledge* will tell you that there is much more to the world than the simple three dimensions we see, and there is a way in which both arguments are true.

Try some simple experiments in psychometry yourself. Hold any object in your hand and ask it questions about its history and the events that have taken place in its presence. Expect your answer to come through one of your normal channels of intuition, clairvoyance, clairaudience, or clairsentience. This is one of the first steps to useful *mediumship* for many students. You could well be one of them.

7. PRECOGNITION

The Bible makes quite a thing out of Pharaoh's dream which Joseph interpreted as predicting seven years of plenty followed by seven years of famine. Joseph's future seemed to be made by his interpretation, but it was *Pharaoh's dream* which we would classify as the precognitive experience. Any feeling, vision, word, or symbol that accurately foretells of a coming event is a manifestation of precognition. Your common sense can often extrapolate from a set of known facts and accurately predict the outcome without your claiming occult powers, but there is a vast gray area beyond the usual bounds of common sense where your E.S.P. can be extremely practical.

Immediately some eager beaver will say, "O.K., tell us who is going to win the feature race at Santa Anita tomorrow." A disinterested medium might be right half of the time, which is excellent in a field of ten or more horses, but there is a joker if you plan to use it for personal profit! When the *something for nothing* motive enters in, we get so bound up in the anxiety born of greed that we block our receipt of the very information we seek.

Nevertheless, there is much good guidance and help for yourself and others to be gained from learning to recognize precognitive tips from spirit. Pay careful attention to your outstanding dreams and the other normal symbols which reach you through your E.S.P. Try to interpret their meaning, but temper your judgment with down-to-earth prudence.

8. SPIRIT PHOTOGRAPHY

There are many examples of spirit entities having their pictures taken beside an unsuspecting member of the family. Such manifestations are classed under the general heading of spirit photography. Some people strive consciously to photograph spirits and consider it a form of mediumship, while others get the manifestations completely by accident. It is definitely true that spirit entities are occasionally photographed.

At one time I tried some simple research in spirit photography, using infrared film in the hope of getting better manifestations. However, it turned out that I got more clearly recognizable results by accident while taking regular pictures of some friends. Now with the power of hindsight, I think I understand the reason. Infrared film is specially sensitive to electromagnetic radiations of lower frequency than visible light bordering on the range of radiant heat. Spirit manifestations must lie in the range of the spectrum on the other side of visible light—somewhere beyond ultraviolet. Therefore, it is easier for them to step down their vibrations to the upper end of the visible spectrum than to further step them down to affect infrared film.

It costs very little to try your hand at spirit photography. Almost everyone has a camera. Ask your spirit friends and teachers to pose for you, then take some pictures. After they are developed, examine the prints carefully for faces or whole bodies that were not physically present during the festivities. You might also examine your old pictures with this thought in mind. A spirit face may have been clearly visible for years, yet ignored because no one had the insight to notice.

9. INDEPENDENT VOICE

As opposed to clairaudience, which is heard only by the medium, there is a phenomenon called independent voice which can be heard by all those present. As you work to develop your psychic centers, thus providing a better instrument for the use of your spirit friends, you may be treated to some interesting bits of this fascinating phenomenon.

A whistle or a simple hello out of nowhere could be the beginning of your new ability. If it appeals to you, ask your teachers for help and keep your ears open. Be sure to respond to spirit greetings of this nature and encourage more. If you should be fortunate enough to combine this with good aura vision, you may talk to visiting spirits just like you talk to your earthly friends when they come to call.

10. SPONTANEOUS PSYCHOKINESIS

This somewhat menacing title is the name given to that class of phenomenon which involves spirit forces lifting or moving physical objects. It is basic human nature to accuse spirits of moving or hiding things. During World War II there were numerous stories told of groups of gremlins whose mischievous antics helped relieve the tensions of the day. But what we are talking about is the physical movement of objects while one or more people are watching.

Obviously things of this nature require better conditions and more spiritual development of the medium than simple clairsentience or intuition, but they are possible if you are willing to work for them.

11. TRUMPET

A fascinating combination of psychokinesis and independent voice results in the phenomenon called trumpet mediumship. The instrument is generally a conical-shaped aluminum tube which resembles a trumpet like the ones used during the Middle Ages. In the presence of the medium, the spirit forces cause the trumpet to levitate and, from the raised position, voices of those from the other side of life speak through the trumpet for all to hear.

Few things give us the appreciation of the power of the spirit world as a good trumpet demonstration. Not many peo-

ple develop these things on their own, and not too many succeed even in good development classes, but this is just as real
as the egg you ate for breakfast.

12. TRANCE

Many spectacular psychic occurrences come from this simple phenomenon. Basically, trance is the temporary surrender
of control of part or all of your physical organism so it can be
used for the manifestation of a spirit entity. Spirits control the
body of the medium, so that the voice quality and mannerisms
exhibited are like the ones they displayed while still living on
Earth, and carry on "normal" conversations with those present.
One should never try to develop trance mediumship without
the presence of a good teacher from the earth life who is familiar with the work, because you will not normally remember
what takes place while you are in trance.

The story of a prominent medium is replete with examples
of the dangers of a good trance medium being exploited by
unscrupulous assistants who direct the manifestations to
achieve their own selfish ends. This story is beautifully told by
Gina Cerminara in her book *Many Mansions*.

A big advantage of trance to the earnest student is the
possibility of receiving lectures directly from highly developed teachers on the spirit side of life. Naturally the trancing
medium will not be able to hear the message firsthand, but
tape recorders can easily catch the lectures for convenient
replay.

13. PLATFORM MEDIUMSHIP

Although it isn't a truly separate type of phenomenon,
platform mediumship deserves a brief word here. To stand
before a group and bring spirit messages of meaning to each
one in turn is an excellent demonstration of the existence of
another dimension beyond the door we call death. When this

work is done sincerely and without pretense, it is one of the better ways of introducing new students to the work.

Probably no two platform mediums work in exactly the same way, but they all use some combination of their basic senses of clairvoyance, clairaudience, and clairsentience. If there is a secret to this work, it is becoming so used to working with the spirit world and so confident they will never let you down, that you completely relax on the platform and let all anxiety or stage fright dissolve in the thrill of loving service to mankind. I have been called upon to give messages in this manner occasionally and, though I don't consider myself really good at it, I feel we should always try to serve. One of my greatest rewards from this activity was the look of bright happiness that appeared on a complete stranger's face the first time I was able to bring through a spirit by name and relationship. When I said, "I am touched by a spirit I feel was your father and I believe his name was Harry," the look on her face was enough living proof of the reality of spirit contact to last us both a lifetime.

Since I had started to study E.S.P. and spirit contact only a few short years before this occurrence, it is my personal opinion that *anyone can develop some degree of this ability,* by the simple art of application of the self with a deep desire to succeed.

14. BILLET READING

Closely akin to platform mediumship is the more spectacular art of blindfold billet reading. Here the members of the audience are requested to write the name of a person in spirit, a question that the spirit should be able to answer, and their name on a small piece of paper generally called a billet. The billets are collected in a basket in plain sight of the audience and deposited on a table in front of the medium. Meanwhile, the medium has been thoroughly blindfolded.

The demonstration starts by the medium picking up a billet and, through psychometry and spirit help, calling out the names and answering the question. Meetings of this nature are also good for opening up the minds of new students to the tremendous power of the spirit world and the advantages we may gain by learning to work with it.

15. ASTRAL TRAVEL

I made several references earlier to out-of-body experiences. It is not uncommon for students to leave their physical bodies in some form of a trance or sleep state and travel with the conscious part of themselves to distant places on Earth or into the spirit realms. The most common name for this is astral travel. What part of you actually travels? It is generally agreed that the emotional body of light, most often called the astral body, is the vehicle which carries the seat of your consciousness on these journeys.

Many of your most vivid dreams are in reality astral experiences, but it is also possible to deliberately leave the body and go to some predetermined place. Think of the time to be saved by attending classes in the spirit world while your physical body lies in bed getting the rest it needs. It would be like recapturing a whole third of your life! Don't scoff. It is within the realm of possibility for all.

16. APPORTS

Spirit has the power to transport physical objects over great distances, virtually instantaneously. Naturally there is as yet no scientific explanation for the process, but it has happened to many people of good integrity. When spirit brings you an object, you have little knowledge of whether it was manufactured in the spirit world or merely brought to you from some distant storage place. In either case we call the object an *apport*. Leland Stanford, the noted patron of Stanford University, collected many apports during his years of serious personal investigation of psychic phenomena. This is a startling, but controversial, manifestation which probably does much more for the faith of the medium than for the audience. After all, it is only the medium who can be absolutely sure that there was no fraud or trickery. Therefore, these demonstrations should be reserved for very carefully screened groups of believers.

17. SPIRIT MATERIALIZATION

Under the proper conditions, a well-developed medium can furnish the physical energy necessary for spirits to manifest in apparently physical bodies. The spirits come in the shape and physical characteristics best known to the person they wish to contact. They can carry on a normal conversation, and may even allow you to touch them on occasion. Once you have seen a spirit aura visiting your home, it is no great stretch of the imagination to visualize this aura forming a force field around which the energy drawn from the medium's body congeals to produce the spirit manifestation. This, too, is a form of phenomenon that has been subject to fraudulent duplication in the past, and it is apt to antagonize those who are not yet ready to understand. It should be demonstrated only to the spiritually prepared few, and then its real purpose should be to serve the spirits who are longing to contact their loved ones directly.

18. OTHER PHENOMENA

We could go on and on and on, but this is hardly the place for it. There are things like levitation of the human body, independent spirit writings on paper or slate, spirit painting and sculpture, and many more. As yet there may be no scientific proof of any of these, but they happen in the daily lives of many sincere students. There is a legend about a lady who asked Edison: "What is electricity?" The great man's answer is said to have been: "Madam, electricity *is,* use it." Certainly this is excellent advice for us. Psychic phenomenon *is,* use it.

How to discover your own advanced phenomena

Now let's come back to you. What does all this mean to you personally? And what might you be doing about it? Let's start way back at the beginning for a moment. The most realistic view of this life is that it is like a day or perhaps a semester in school. You have certain lessons to learn and special tasks to accomplish along the way. Your achievements during this session of life-school will benefit you both now and in future classes to come. Like earthly children in grammar school, we can make it hard or easy for ourselves by our attitude and the extent of application of our efforts to the tasks at hand.

Now, as regards the subject of psychic phenomena, the proper use of some phases will undoubtedly help you in your life's mission. The better your working knowledge, the better you will be equipped to learn and grow. You entered this life with definite natural aptitudes for handling the specific types of phenomena which will be most useful in accomplishing your mission. Some of us may develop a great many variations while others will seem limited to just a few; but there is something for everybody. Certainly the more you open your mind, the more useful these things will become to you. Your sincere, open attitude can help lift up the consciousness of all mankind.

How do you look for your hidden talents in this field? First, as always, is your developing sensitivity to notice the tiny or subtle manifestations of spirit that take place all around you every day. In simple words, *pay attention!* We can't put enough emphasis on this simple technique—*pay attention*. A basic law of nature is that attention always elicits response, and this is greatly amplified in the psychic fields. As you notice the little knocks on your wall, say "Hi, you're very welcome here" to the spirit and you will be amazed at how much more frequently they will come. Be on the lookout for spirit auras and greet them all. You wouldn't ignore a physical body coming to call on you, and your spirit friends are equally real. Why snub them?

It has been said in every major religion, "As you turn to God, God turns to you." This is another manifestation of the law of response. Your spirit teachers are the angelic ambassadors of God sent to help you. Certainly the more attention you give them, the greater response you can expect. Take your earnest desire into your quiet place and ask your teachers to help you continually improve your contact with them. React with a thank-you to their exhilarating touch or the small symbol of greeting that is certain to reach you. Then ask for guidance and help in unfolding your psychic abilities.

Begin a campaign to open your mind. Get books on E.S.P. and the psychic world from your library and *study* them. Visit as many different types of psychic demonstrations as you can find, and seek to fully understand the principles behind each. You will naturally meet people who like to talk about these things, and you can learn a great deal in this manner. You may be invited to join a development class which can be an important step in achieving things like trance, trumpet, and platform mediumship. But here your down-to-earth good judgment is necessary. There are many deeply spiritual people teaching in this field, but unfortunately there are also quacks and pirates. Know what you are getting into *before you do it.* Particularly if you are contemplating trance, or any phenomenon where you surrender temporary control of your physical organism, be sure that all sessions are attended by a close friend or relative who can tell you exactly what happened while you were gone.

Do everything possible to put yourself at ease while you are seeking, whether it be in your own quiet place or in a good class. Nothing drives spirit demonstrations away like your own anxiety. One student was in a development class working for trumpet. For nine weeks she had some interesting visions and guidance, but no physical manifestations. Then toward the end of the tenth meeting, her trumpet raised slightly and seemed to emit a low growl. She became so excited that she jumped up, grabbed the instrument, and looked inside. This anxious action completely broke the vibration, and for many weeks the trumpet remained still and silent.

The same relaxed awareness that gave you the first glimpse of the world of your spirit teachers is the catalyst for any advanced development you may desire. Take it with you, wherever you go!

Concentrate your efforts on one simple phenomenon at a time

It seems that all spiritual work is a lesson in patience. We are like children in these matters, doing silly things like standing back to back to compare heights as we grow, and always wishing we had achieved everything already. This is the point to pause and renew your oneness with the Infinity of Creation. To the Infinite Being divisions of time and space are meaningless nonsense since He is all time and all space already. The better your feeling of oneness, the easier it will be to control your impatience. But here in our finite world, it is best to tackle one job at a time, even in the realm of spirit manifestations.

A little communion with your teachers in quiet meditation will help you choose the particular type of manifestation which is most likely to come to you in the beginning. Then really try to develop it. Ask your spirit teachers for help, and regularly apply your psychic energies and conscious attention to a development program.

One student decided that she would do best by striving for the development of aura vision. In her quiet place, she asked for advice as to method and for help in unfolding this psychic faculty. Quickly the idea came to look for her own aura first. She brought a large mirror into her meditation area with the idea that she might stare at the area around her head, then close her eyes and possibly get an after-image of her aura. The process got slightly short-circuited when she stared at her head for a few moments and noticed a faint fringe of light around it. At first the light seemed to come and go, and she wondered if her eyes were playing tricks on her. But a few days' practice taught her that the trick was in the *way* she looked at herself in the mirror. If she kept her eyes focused right on the center of her forehead while she looked at the area around the edges, her aura seemed to stand out very clearly.

The beauty of aura vision is that it can be practiced almost anytime and anywhere. Our student soon found that she could spot the aura of people clear across a big room, or even walking down the street. Alone without a mirror, she could practice looking at the aura around her fingers, arms, and feet. There is a whole new science of human aura waiting to be unfolded for the healing and educational benefit of mankind. Dedicated students like this one will one day bring it forth to the world.

The degree of *application* to your development work makes all the difference. We still live in a material world that makes its special demands on our time for the earning of our keep and for the fulfillment of our previously contracted earthly obligations. To shirk any of these is to fall backwards spiritually as well as materially. Seek your own point of balance that does a good job of satisfying the world's demands but leaves you the maximum time for spiritual striving.

The recapture of just half the time you usually waste or fritter away will give you progress that is richly rewarding. An excellent period for affirmative prayer is the time spent driving or riding to work. Many psychic exercises lend themselves to practice while you are actually working. There is plenty of time to handle everything without neglecting your family *if you want it that way.* There is an old saying that if you want a job accomplished quickly, give it to a busy person to perform. You will always accomplish just as much as you honestly set out to do—no more, and certainly no less. Do it!

How to seek spontaneous phenomena

The idea of *seeking* something *spontaneous* contains a seemingly intellectual conflict quite similar to some of the basics of Zen Buddhism. From the lessons of Zen we may also find the help we seek. Anyone who claims to understand it, doesn't!

Zen is not capable of comprehension by the mind because it is an experience completely outside the realm of finite thought. Thus, in seeking Satori, the intellect plays a very subordinate role, much like a servant preparing the master's house to receive a welcome guest. This servant knows not when the guest will come, or what he looks like, but he perseveres and is eventually rewarded with the privilege of serving the guest personally.

So it is with spontaneous phenomena. We can play the role of the servant and prepare for its coming to the best of our ability, but we cannot of ourselves bring it to pass. The Zen monk doesn't refuse to work for Satori just because his intellect and physical body are not able to control it. He knows that the experience is worth all the perseverance he can muster. Similarly, we should never refuse or give up our seeking of the truly spontaneous phenomena. But how do we seek?

Once again, you must start with your steadily developing relaxed awareness. Take it to your quiet place and talk the matter over with your teachers. Ask for spontaneous psychic manifestations to be directed to you by the spirit world. Earnestly desire an ever-improving rapport with spirit, and communicate it to your teachers as the reason you are interested in phenomena. Check your attitude carefully and often. Are you still looking for something for nothing? Are you seeking thrills or parlor game type entertainment? Work to purge your being of any traces of such negative attitudes.

There are only two good reasons to seek spirit phenomena, and both should be present before you can expect results. First is simple friendship, the warm love that makes people want to enjoy each other's company; and the other is a desire for that cooperation which encourages mutual spiritual growth. The sideshow artists may always be with us, but their shallow results fall infinitely short of the product of friendship and cooperation. Constant policing of your attitude, and maintenance of your relaxed awareness, are your contributions as the humble servant waiting for the arrival of the invited guest.

As little demonstrations begin to take place around you, consciously direct your mental and psychic powers to amplify the spirit signals. It is normal and necessary for your spirit friends to borrow physical energy from you in order to produce their manifestations. Your relaxed and willing cooperation will materially assist the development of regular and frequent demonstrations of the presence of spirit entities.

A small group of seekers gathered in their host's living room one warm Sunday afternoon. During a lull in the conversation, someone said, "Gee, it's hot! Why don't we open a window?" Before anyone could move, a window opened by itself, and no physical body was within six feet of it at the time! Though startled, the host said, "Thank you, good spirit, now please join us in our discussions." Then each person, in turn, was touched by a spirit hand in greeting; and the conversation continued, much uplifted by this simple spirit manifestation.

Children are often richly blessed by spirit companionship, and we should be alert to avoid the adult tendency to teach them that such things are impossible. A spiritually minded young mother thought she heard an unusual amount of laughter coming from her small son's room. She walked softly to the door and peeked in. He seemed to be playing ball with something or somebody his mother couldn't see, so she walked quietly back to her kitchen. Presently the boy came looking for his mother. To her question, "What were you doing in there that was so much fun?" he answered, "Oh, I was just playing with one of my friends." Because she accepted this answer with understanding, it was a beautiful experience for both mother and son.

A young couple became acquainted with these manifestations through spirit activation of a little joke. One night at bedtime, instead of getting up to turn out the lamp, the husband waved his hand at it and said, "Poof." Instantly the light went out, and they laughed at the coincidence. But next morning the lamp worked perfectly and the bulb was not burned out. On the second night the wife said, "Let me try it this time. Poof."

And sure enough the light went out again. They laughed and agreed the bulb must be burned out this time. But again the next morning the light burned and the switch worked perfectly. On the third night the "poof" worked again, so they decided to take the hint and begin a serious study of psychic phenomena. The lamp functioned quite normally for years afterwards, but their seeking led them to many interesting experiences.

How to approach the direction of phenomena

The slightest taste of spontaneous psychic phenomena seems to whet one's appetite for more, and very quickly there grows a desire to produce it at will. In other words, you suddenly realize that you urgently desire the ability to produce at least some form of phenomena whenever it seems appropriate. Before there is much chance for real progress along these lines, it is again necessary to police your motivations. The question is, why do you want to produce phenomena? When and where would you want to use them?

We are quick to rationalize our inner motives and tell ourselves that these desires are purely for the spiritual advancement of mankind. But are they really? Earlier I mentioned my first out-of-body experience wherein I seemed to have the power of levitation. My reaction the next morning was: "Wow, if I can only learn to do that in the flesh, I can fill the Hollywood Bowl with people and really open their eyes!" What's wrong with such a well-meaning attitude? Simply that the statement was a good rationalization of a not-so-good desire for fame and fortune by creating a sensation. It's very hard to get rid of the selfishness and little ego that would willingly exploit the psychic for personal gain. That sort of sensationalism would close more minds than it opened, and create all sorts of wild controversy and skepticism. There is certainly a place for the more startling phenomena, but that is in small classes of truly dedicated students who will understand the real meaning of such things, give thanks, and talk about it only among people who will not be affronted. Be sure you understand the reasons behind your desires, and purify them before you seek.

O.K., now you are convinced you have cleansed your attitude of all selfishness. How do we start? It is necessary to provide some reasonably appropriate physical facilities. For some time you have been using a favorite quiet place. Let's examine it in detail to see if it can also be suitable for a place to develop phenomena. An ideal place would meet these special requirements:

1. It will be absolutely quiet while you are using it.
2. It can be locked from the inside to prevent your being interrupted.
3. It is equipped with some sort of blackout curtains so you can exclude all light when necessary.
4. It is supplied with a comfortable chair and a small table which can be used as an altar. The altar may contain two candles in holders, incense, incense burner, a mirror, and anything else that appeals to your esthetic sense.

Let's call this place your *meditation chamber* to distinguish it from any convenient location you may use for a quiet place. Prepare your meditation chamber for use by lighting the candles and incense, then lock the door to insure against interruptions. It is good to open with the Lord's Prayer, Psalm 23, or both; then call on your spirit teachers and ask for their presence, their protection, and their help. Now tell your teachers the specific purpose of your meditation. Let's say you want to develop automatic writing and promise to join them regularly for this purpose. All that remains is to mentally direct your subconscious faculties to assist in the phenomenon, pick up your pencil and assume a comfortable writing position, then remain relaxed and patient until you get results.

Directed phenomena in the darkness

If you want a seed to sprout and grow, it is normal to plant it in carefully prepared soil. There in the darkness of the loving mother earth, something triggers the growth process and the seed comes to active life, putting down roots and soon sending a sprout upwards to seek the sunlight. For some reason not yet clearly understood by the human mind, the development of many forms of psychic phenomena must also begin in complete darkness, symbolic of the little seed planted in mother earth.

Trumpet, trance, spirit materializations, apports, and the like specifically require nearly total darkness during your development period. If you have any inclination or tendency toward trance, you should arrange to be accompanied in your chamber by someone you trust implicitly. Also a tape recorder would be very useful so you can carefully review the discourses which come through your physical organism while you are away in trance.

Now let's go back to your meditation chamber, light the candles and incense, lock the door, and adjust the blackout to exclude all light from the outside. It is probably a good idea to have a trumpet on hand whether that is your primary interest or not. These little instruments are advertised at very nominal prices in any psychic periodical. Open with a prayer, then call your teachers and tell them that this is your regular period to sit for psychic development. Then extinguish the candles and sit quietly in the darkness.

This is not the time to be so insistent on one special phenomenon that you reject others which may begin to come. You will probably be visited by tiny lights, and often by a whistle or the calling of your name. This is also an excellent place for the further unfoldment of your clairvoyance, clairaudience, and clairsentience. Be receptive to whatever manifestations your teachers are able to bring, and respond with thanksgiving for each one. Sincerity, patience, and perseverance are your contribution to this development process. Your spirit teachers will furnish the rest.

A woman sat in the dark for psychic development and was taken on an out-of-body trip to a classroom in the spirit world. She attended a fascinating lecture on reincarnation, and at its conclusion she was shown a small silver cross that was to be a spirit gift as a memento of the experience. When she returned to her body she was delighted to find a small silver cross on her altar, exactly like the one she had been shown by the spirit teacher.

You will never be fully aware of the fantastic power of the spirit world until you experience it personally. Start sitting for psychic development now.

Directed phenomena in the light

It will be a time of great happiness when you are able to bring your newly developed psychic abilities out of the darkness into the world of light. You can't help but derive real satisfaction from demonstrating psychic and spirit contact to the little groups of believers you contact along the way. Our civilization needs many more dedicated workers to help in the task of opening the collective mind to the true relationship of our physical world to the world of spirit, and to the universal scheme of things.

There is much new philosophy waiting for the time when man can open his heart to its teachings of the *reality of the brotherhood of all beings* and our direct relationship to the Creator. As you become more adept at demonstrating psychic phenomena, it is important that you understand the responsibility that comes with it. Because you can demonstrate the truth of principles which the average individual only vaguely suspects, you have become a special ambassador of God to everyone you contact. From now on, it is not just your psychic demonstrations that will be observed, but the sum total of *everything that is you*.

It is imperative that you accept your new responsibility and strive to live a life of true inspiration to all. Yes, you are still a human being with human faults and weaknesses, but those within your sphere of influence will be apt to forget that fact. To them you are an ambassador of God and the spirit world, and their concept of God will be greatly influenced by everything you seem to stand for. As a practical matter, there remains much pettiness and bigotry in our world, and more than your share will undoubtedly come your way. Accept your responsibility as a spiritual leader and rise above such things.

Our Master Teacher left us the simple ground rules: Resist not evil, turn the other cheek and *If thy brother trespass against thee, rebuke him; and if he repent, forgive him.* How many times? *Forgive him unto seventy times seven!* This is not to suggest that you become a spineless jellyfish who is afraid to stand up for what you believe, but it is an effective way of minimizing the strife and vexation around you. It is clearly a matter of good judgment of the importance of a problem to the spiritual well-being of you, the group, and the community, whether you shall grab a whip and drive the money changers out of the temple, or smile and turn the other cheek.

You are here to be about the Father's business. As you seek to live your life in that manner, you will receive all the guidance and help necessary to your effectiveness. *Let your light so shine before men that they may see your good works, and glorify your Father which is in heaven.*

POINTS TO REMEMBER

I. The humility born of deep mystical understanding is a practical prerequisite to advanced psychic phenomena.

II. You may expect many different types of phenomena. For example: knocks and raps, aura vision, automatic writing, inspirational writing, inspirational lecturing, psychometry, precognition, spirit photography, independent voice, spontaneous psychokinesis, trumpet, trance, platform mediumship, billet reading, astral travel, apports, spirit materializations, and many more.

III. Seek to unfold your own advanced phenomena as part of your overall spiritual development program.

IV. Phenomena are not for thrills or parlor games.

V. It is useful to prepare a meditation chamber that can be locked from the inside to be certain you are not disturbed during your development work.

VI. You will become an ambassador of God to all mankind. Accept your responsibility.

how to
Insure Your
New Growth

Those who have read my book, *The Miraculous Laws of Universal Dynamics,* already understand that this book is really *Volume II* of a series, and it constitutes our third trip around the evolutionary spiral. We closed *Volume I* with a suggested method of beginning your new growth by scientific prayer for the manifestation of an organization to fill the gaping void between science and religion.

Throughout life we see evidence of the spiral of evolution. Radio is a simple illustration. It began by the use of a plain little gadget, the old-fashioned crystal, until it was replaced by the more complicated vacuum tube. We returned to the use of the crystal, now renamed transistor, in honor of its greatly increased effectiveness. We returned to the old concept, but a whole revolution higher on the evolutionary spiral. From technology to dress styles to morals, things seem to progress in a spiral rather than a straight line, and the same is true of our spiritual progress. We continually return to the old ways, but with deeper understanding born of our more extensive experience. Even the apparently unresolvable conflict between modern science and religion will melt away as we travel the spiral onward to a new living religion based not on blind dogmatic faith, but on enlightened understanding of the inner meaning of the old teachings. We will approach God with a fuller measure of knowledge than the generations who were asked to accept on blind faith. In our time, faith can come to mean *certainty,* not merely hope or wavering trust. Let's take a better look at the apparent conflict.

Science vs. religion

Blind faith may have been a good vehicle for the population of 2,000 years ago, but our contemporary society has taught us to prize something else. The scientific method is the vogue, and its tool is the intellect. But we must manage to view science in its proper perspective. Just what is it? What are its limitations? And why should we worship the intellect more than some other tool, like a hammer or a saw?

A high school teacher might open his elementary class by defining science as the systematic classification of knowledge obtained by study, experimentation, and practice. This is a good working definition, *if* you understand that *knowledge* is neither static nor sacred. Science constantly seeks now knowledge, and reclassifies the old in the light of that which comes later. But isn't this just another form of growth? Isn't today's knowledge merely yesterday's speculative ideas proved true? And aren't today's truths often discovered to be but special cases of greater truths?

A good example of unfolding knowledge lies in the history of geometry. It started with Euclidean plane geometry. Here were evolved the basic concepts of the point, the line, the plane, and the various plane figures such as the triangle, circle, and polygon. Then came the addition of another dimension. Plane geometry was conceived to be merely a special case of spherical geometry, still true but only as it approximates a point on a sphere. Then a whole new set of higher principles evolved to explain the world more nearly as it is. Thus it made possible theories of navigation which *practically benefited* travel of all kinds. In the same way, Professor Einstein showed that physics as it was known is true, but only at relative speeds which are insignificant with respect to the speed of light.

Not all concepts of science stand the test of time as well as Euclidean geometry and elementary physics. The batting average is pretty good because the theories are based on the observation of actual phenomena, but scientists are quite human and capable of making mistakes. Even the collective group of specialties referred to as science is capable of making whopping big mistakes!

Less than five centuries ago the majority of the scientific community still believed our world to be flat. True, the Greek civilization, B.C., knew the world to be a sphere but that would be small comfort to Columbus if Queen Isabella had refused to back him. There have been many more recently accepted theories which seem utterly absurd by the measure of late twentieth-century knowledge. We won't belabor the point, but a couple of good examples are worth laughing about.

Less than three centuries ago Georg Ernst Stahl expounded a theory of combustion which was generally accepted by the scientific community for nearly a hundred years. In this conception a material of fire, which Stahl named *phlogiston,* is lost by every combustible in the process of burning. Phlogiston plausibly, but quite inaccurately, explained the process now called *oxidation and reduction,* as well as the heat given off by the animal body and its restoration by food. The discovery of the element oxygen ultimately led to the abandonment of the phlogiston concept; but the theory was so firmly established that oxygen was first called "dephlogisticated air." How many bright and shiny scientific theories of today will vanish with phlogiston into the archives of the dead past? Only time will tell, but we can be sure the number is greater than most people realize.

From the time of the death of phlogiston, well into the twentieth century, the theory of *ether* has waxed and waned in scientific popularity. Ether was a hypothetical substance occupying all space, including that filled by solid matter, and serving to transmit any of the forces which one material object exerts upon another from a *distance.* As sound is propagated by vibrations in the air, so light, gravity, and magnetism were theorized to be propagated by vibrations in ether. Stated in its simplest form, sound is to air as light, gravity, and magnetism are to ether. For the whole of the nineteenth century and well into our own time, ether reigned as the best explanation of the related phenomena. It was not until Albert Einstein showed that many of the properties ascribed to ether could just as well be attributed to empty space and time, that the theory was seriously challenged. Ether is generally in disrepute today, but that whole realm of science is in a state of flux and it wouldn't seriously stretch the imagination to see the old theory return to prominence—but with the term *ether* replaced by a fancy new name, like transistor instead of crystal.

This discussion is not intended as a slap at either science or religion. It is simply an attempt to provide some historical perspective. In the short run, science can be as dogmatic as the most intolerant religion, but time has its ways of bringing out truth. It is logical to respect both science and religion for the good that they accomplish, but it's also prudent to keep each in the best possible perspective.

Science and religion look at matter

The ancient Greeks conceived of matter as composed of tiny solid particles, reasoning that if you start to divide a piece of any substance, you can continue to divide it into smaller and smaller parts until finally you will reach the smallest particle, which will prove indivisible. They named this hypothetical smallest particle the *atom*.

Antedating the Greeks, but persisting in an unbroken line to this day, some "mystery schools" and religious orders taught that matter is merely a form of energy. They were laughed at by scientists for many centuries. The discovery of radium with its curious property of radiation gave a faint inkling that these way-out people might have a point. But it took the atom bomb to prove them right.

Even in the 1930s, an atom was a relatively simple thing made up of arrangements of only three basic particles: the very light, fast-moving, negatively charged *electron;* the dense, positively charged *proton;* and the dense, electrically neutral *neutron*. However, a little stranger soon began to make itself known in atomic circles. It was light and fast like an electron, but it carried a positive charge. It didn't fit very well into their neat little atoms, so the scientists politely labeled it a *positron* and hoped that if they ignored it, it would go away. But instead of going, it brought along its whole family; so today the number of recognized atomic particles is well over a dozen and threatening to continue to increase.

Of special interest to the layman is the concept of anti-particles and antimatter. Modern physics now tells us that each atomic particle has an exactly opposite counterpart. It seems conceivable to our scientists that an atom of regular matter could collide with an atom of antimatter and the result would be some sort of explosion, with the two atoms canceling each other out, leaving nothing, as in algebraic addition. There has even been scientific speculation of whole galaxies of antimatter in outer space, and the possible results of their collision with regular galaxies.

An article on antimatter provokes me to a little tongue-in-cheek scientific speculation. If we look upon *nothing* as being made up of equal parts of matter and un-matter (a more convenient term than antimatter), we are able to produce the first completely scientific explanation of the miracle of the loaves and fishes:

Jesus stood on the mountainside wishing to feed the hungry multitude, but He had *nothing* except a few scrawny fish with which to supply them. Being a Man of great understanding, He used a fish for a pattern and divided His *nothing* into equal parts of fish and un-fish. Having no particular use for the un-fish, He threw them away and fed the multitude with the regular fish; and so also with the bread. Facetious? Of course, but it still leaves much food for thought.

Only as man uses his creative imagination does he gain new insight into the true nature of the world around him. This imagination has built excellent machines and devices to extend the useful range of our senses; but we must take care not to let them restrict our thinking to the dead part of our objective environment.

Your new beginning is your contribution to the world's future

The promise of the future is always the evolution of man's knowledge, the continuing improvement of scientific techniques and gadgetry leading to an ever-greater scientific understanding of the universe. Even scientific history has a way of repeating itself, like the spiral from crystal to vacuum tube to transistor. Where is this scientific spiral of growth leading us? Eventually and inevitably back to God at a wonderful new level of understanding.

Enough progress has been made that we are nearing a major breakthrough toward the union of science and religion. Out of this union will grow the new beginning of peace and cooperation between all beings of the Earth. Right now there is a significant opportunity for a few people to make a very special contribution to this important phase of the progress of man. The breakthrough is inevitable. It is bound to happen sooner or later. But think of the untold suffering and anguish that could be spared many millions of human beings if this union of science and religion can be achieved fifty or a hundred years sooner than by accidental fallout from our space and defense programs.

This brings us back to the conclusion of *The Miraculous Laws of Universal Dynamics* where I suggested the need for a new kind of organization, "a living, vibrant group unhampered by the rigors of academic pressure and the strict scientific approach or the doctrines and dogma of traditional religion."

We briefly sketched the mission of such a group, and I invited the reader to join in prayer for his own progress and the birth of the group. It concluded with this suggested twice daily affirmation: "I trust in God with all my heart and He directs my growth in the Christ Idea. He is giving birth to an effective organization to unite science and religion into a living, vibrant organism, now. Thank you, Heavenly Father, for this perfect gift to mankind."

Your new beginning of spiritual accomplishment in E.S.P.

Balance is necessary even for spiritual growth and achievement. The ancient occult teachings tell us that we should strive in three specific areas to attain balanced growth. They are (1) work for personal growth and progress, (2) work for the progress of your organization or school, and (3) work for the progress of all mankind. Your progress is inextricably bound up with the progress of all life on this planet. You provide the best spiritual growth for yourself when you strive also for the good of mankind through the vehicle of some organization or school whose aims and beliefs are consistent with your own.

Note that number one is always your personal growth. Nothing will ever relieve you of the basic responsibility for developing the potential of your own individuality! That must ever be your underlying goal. In a very practical sense, the submergence of your individual goal in earnest work for the good of all mankind is the best path to personal attainment. Naturally the sensible way to work for the advancement of mankind is through an organization. There are many worthwhile schools through which you can serve. Choose any one that appeals to you, but *do work with one or more of them!* It will be to your own greatest advantage.

Your prayers are important!

The Great Wall of China stands as a magnificent example of what can be accomplished by group perseverance. It was fashioned out of determination, stick-to-it-iveness, guts, and very little else. But it will live forever as a monument to the potential of *group effort*. No member of any group or school can ever be more important than you, because it is only the accumulated efforts of everyone that adds up to results.

POINTS TO REMEMBER

I. All life is a spiral of evolution.

II. The apparent conflict of science and religion is the result of lack of historical perspective.

III. Creative imagination is the source of all material progress.

IV. The promise of the future is a breakthrough that will unite science and religion into one vibrant, spiritual organism.

V. Balanced growth comes from working for the progress of yourself, your school, and all mankind.

Major Problem-Solving to Start a Fresh New Life with E.S.P.

Now 33 delightful years later I took a look at what before was our closing chapter, Chapter 11. I still like it and agree with it. And it still works! Better and better! We'll start with a personal example, knowing that you can do it too, as in *These works that I do, shall ye do also and even greater works shall ye do.* Quite in that tradition, while the original of this book was being print-ed, spirit helped us solve a bunch of problems, thus bringing us the manifestation of our "dream" organization to stand between science and religion, throw a rope to each and bring them to unity. We did it as a church, *E.S.P. Laboratory,* and dutifully set out upon our mission. Let's start with a bit of his-tory for background, then get to the "How to's" that will work for you.

Spirit divided the mission into two logical sections: *The Scientific and Semiscientific* approach and *The Religious and Occult* approach. Since the gadgetry is so interesting and so much fun, let's take the scientific part first.

Dr. J. B. Rhine assaults the scientific community and shows that seriousness is a disadvantage to psychic activities

Dr. J. B. Rhine, then at Duke University, designed a series of experiments to prove the existence of what he accurately called Extrasensory Perception as an easier-to-understand term than the earlier one, Psi Phenomena. He later moved on to his own foundation and continued to work on scientific proofs for many years. To me his most significant contribution to the whole scientific part was his comment on the value of humor in E.S.P. work. The early studies were boring indeed—hours of sitting there tossing coins, rolling dice, glaring at cards, and the like. He noted that as boredom set in, the students' scores would tend to drop, but with the injection of a bit of humor, like: "If you get a good score this time, I'll buy you a beer," the scores tended to pick right up. A lesson to remember, which we finally carried all the way to our concept of the happy, winning life as a 25-hour/day, 8-day/week Spirit Party. Much more on this later. But let me interject our Spirit Mentor, Pan's definition of seriousness: "A subtle camouflage of abject fear—the fear of failure." Let's let that sink in for awhile as we look at some of the world's progress.

The scientific and semiscientific approach

Naturally this turned us to what is called Radionics. The idea is to use machines, or some sort of physical paraphernalia, to gather, direct, and control what we might best call the psychic energies that naturally flow in and through your body's *chakras* or psychic centers. The string of devices belonged to Abrahms, Ruth Drown (who died in prison because the FDA claimed her gadget was fraudulent), DeLawar in England, and Hieronymous (whom I met in person for instruction), whose gadget was granted a U.S. patent by being disguised as a way of computing atomic weight. All of these devices were somehow dependent upon a "touch plate" so the operator could tune the device until he got the "shtick" or a seeming magnetic force that stopped one's hand as it was rubbing the touch plate and indicated that the tuning was complete. The kicker to this work was when it was demonstrated that a circuit drawing of the device would work just as well as the physical gadget itself. I'll let you ponder the psychic/spiritual significance and practical value of that one while we look at several other examples.

Orgone vs. the Odic Force

Baron Reichenbach was thrown out of the German Academy of Sciences in the late 1800s for his advocacy of the "Odic Force." He grew green plants in a totally dark basement by using an above-ground antenna and a wire that "piped" the essence of the sunlight into the dark area. It worked, the plants flourished, and, as he said, the energy followed the normal laws of electricity. To this day I believe that this is a viable force needing more study to make its uses more practical. At least he just got ejected from the Academy. Our next subject, Willhelm Reich, was another who died in prison because the FDA declared his devices fraudulent.

Reich's device was what he called "Orgone," another interesting form of energy. It was "generated" by alternate layers of metal and plastic forming an Orgone Box. The big ones were for patients to sit in and experience healing, but when misused the energy could be devastating. Smaller versions were used for magick and all sorts of fun experiments. At E.S.P. Lab we tried to combine the Odic and Orgone forces, but they seemed to cancel each other out like the carrier wave is canceled out in modern radio. We'll examine this phenomenon more closely as we discuss the following.

The miracle of pyramid energy

The book *Psychic Discoveries Behind the Iron Curtain* provided an interesting series of links between science and religion, pyramid energy being the most spectacular. I had just barely heard of the book when a friend brought me a 6-inch scale model of the Great Pyramid with the suggestion that I play with it. The Russians used these to sharpen razor blades, and credited them with the ability to preserve matter in something like a mummified form. My instant reaction was: "This should be a super-good thoughtform incubator!" In order to make sense out of this for you, we need to switch or bridge to the Religious and Occult approach.

The religious and occult approach: thoughtforms nurtured by pyramid energy

Any well-formed idea is a living energy field. I learned this from my study of the human aura or energy field that surrounds or, better, *is* part of your physical body. It's easy to see aura when you understand that this is really self-luminous energy that can be brought into focus by using your peripheral or night vision capabilities. My lookout training in the Navy in World War II made this a cinch, but you can develop it almost instantly—just sit in front of a mirror and focus your "normal" vision on the center of your forehead right above the eyes and very quickly the bright aura around your head will seem to pop out in your peripheral vision. Don't try to look at it directly or it will seem to disappear, but it's *always* there.

The reason for this little digression was to explain the nature of a thoughtform. In Theosophy they talk about a "floating thoughtform" as a fully developed idea. Conveniently my office in my then-aerospace job looked out on a line of design draftsmen. I often gazed at them while they worked, and enjoyed watching their auras. Pretty soon I noticed the formation of thoughtforms within their auras. A fellow would be drawing along and when he finished a section, he'd lean back for a moment and the thoughtform would indeed detach itself and float away to begin its task of manifestation in the three-dimensional world. Fantastic!

Using the power while recognizing the danger of the pyramid as a thoughtform incubator

Metaphysical affirmations with visualization always create living thoughtforms. I like to tease that the only difference between a metaphysician and a "white magickian" is that the magickian builds his thoughtforms deliberately and thus has better control of the project. So at E.S.P. Lab we were building thoughtforms just as you can today, then seeking to incubate them to make them stronger and more able to manifest. We had tried a bassinet with the thoughtforms placed in the cute hollow eggs that ladies' pantyhose came in, and loved and chanted over them every day until we felt like turning them loose to manifest. The pyramid did prove to be a much better place to incubate thoughtforms because it magnified or enhanced the energy. But look out! It magnifies the emotional energy, *not* the wording of the thoughtform. You can do this quite easily yourself, but beware.

My original experience should serve as an excellent example. The Lab was very young and money was extremely tight as is normal with nonprofit entities. So I decided to try creating a thoughtform to generate money. More or less tongue-in-cheek, I built a thoughtform for $150 extra in the next day's incoming mail. Fantastic! It manifested. So, I thought, I wonder if this is just coincidence, let's give it another try. This time I went for an extra $300. It took two days this time but it did manifest nicely. Now the psychic atmosphere changed. I got dollar signs where my eyeballs should have been. Full of greed and avarice I did another thoughtform, this time for $1,000. The pyramid dutifully multiplied my anxiety and put me to bed with an awful migraine for two whole days. What a lesson! When it's fun, it works; when it's serious or uptight, it backfires! This was another lesson on the road to our 25-hour/day, 8-day/week Spirit Party.

By the way, you can easily make your own model pyramid for research or play. Just get a hunk of posterboard and cut out four isosceles triangles, 9⅜ inches on the base and 8⅞ inches on the sides. These will go together to make a perfect 6-inch high pyramid. Regular adhesive tape will do nicely for the seams and it's fun to decorate them to your own taste. We used to sell them but decided that was silly since they're so easy for you to make for yourself.

How to understand and practically use the pyramid energy

We were doing regular trance work back then to learn more about how much and how far your Spirit People can help you. So we posed the question to my original trance mentor, Professor Reinhardt: "Can you tell us more of the nature of the pyramid energy as it applies to us on the practical level?" His response was quite in point. First came the explanation that visible light is just one octave in the electromagnetic spectrum, which includes radio waves, higher frequency carrier waves for TV, to hotter infrared waves through visible light to ultraviolet with an unlimited beyond. He next said that if you consider that the human body and its psychic centers, or chakras, could be represented as a rainbow with red at the root center all the way to violet at the crown center, we may liken this to the musical key of C, then the pyramid would be in the key of E flat. We calculated quickly that this put the color blue at the one-third level of the king's chamber, which is traditionally called the healing level. And we've always considered blue the color of the healing energy.

So for practical application purposes we already told you how to build your pyramid. Now build a little platform to put your about-to-be thoughtform at one-third of the way up from the bottom of your pyramid—2 inches should do it. Next build your thoughtform. Write while you visualize the desired goal (as "a major windfall of money for me," "a good new job," "a wonderful new lover," or whatever is your immediate goal) on a small piece of paper. Hold it between the palms of your hands while you do the quickie E.S.P. development exercise as given in Chapter 1. Then place it tenderly on the platform and cover it with your pyramid, taking care to orient it so that one side is facing true magnetic north. Whenever you feel like it, you might add to the energy by chanting a bit while facing the north side of the pyramid. I like to use chants for this from my book *Helping Yourself with White Witchcraft*—here's a very good one:

Rama, Agni, send the Light to me,
Rama, Agni, send the lush Green Light to me.
Bathe me with your growth and love,
Send abundance from above,
Rama, Agni, send the Light that sets me free.

It's sort of a tradition to release the thoughtform by fire (meaning to burn that little piece of paper) to turn the whole project over to your Spirit and Nature Spirit Friends to be nurtured to full manifestation.

C. G.'s early results from the pyramid work

C. G., one of my former students, paid a call at my office to report: "Al, I found out you really do have to be careful about how you word your thoughtform request, as well as your mood when doing the planting. I planted one worded 'Let there be a $1,000 windfall for me.' Next morning I was parked in front of my house about to leave for work when I was rear-ended, got a mild whiplash, and the net settlement was $1,000."

We pretty much agreed to begin anything like this with "Let there be no harm to anyone. . . ." Interestingly enough, he had several more successes before the novelty and fun wore off and his seriousness stopped his progress for awhile. Do keep this in mind in any of your psychic or magickal endeavors—my pet line here is: Make it fun and win *big*!

Past-life studies—reincarnation made practical

Colorful comebacks in an interview situation can be fun. One of my favorites is when the interviewer asks: "Do you believe in reincarnation?" I'll invariably say: "No. But I don't believe in breathing either; I just have to do it." In one of his many books Brad Steiger called me one of America's leading trance mediums, because of the over-1,500 past-life readings I did for people over a seven-year period. My spirit mentor, Professor Reinhardt, handled the trances and I teased him many a time that if I woke up speaking in a thick German accent, he was out of here! He always gave me my body back whole, but I finally discontinued that kind of trance work because past lives are generally very boring. However, there are still many benefits to be gained by what we call past-life regression. Later, I'll give you a simple technique for do-it-yourself past-life exploration for fun and profit, but first let's have a look at some direct benefits.

Past-life exploration as research for a new book

It started out as an experimental class in past-life regression—almost as boring as the trance work, but once in awhile we hit pay dirt! Our group was about 20 students meeting weekly at the old E.S.P. Lab building in Los Angeles, and pretty regularly we began to see beautiful old ritual work that we were doing back then. We brought it forward, dusted it off, and tried it—and it worked! This turned out to be the research for my book *Helping Yourself with White Witchcraft*, which is still in print and available from Prentice Hall since its publication in 1972.

We also learned to look to past lives for the root causes of chronic maladies in the here and now. For instance, I had a pretty serious migraine problem. I went into past lives specifically to find out what may have come forward to cause them. Sure enough, I lost a body to the water-torture treatment in fourteenth-century China (this was substantiated by a class member who said that this particular time period was the heyday of the water-torture era), to a later execution by the Spanish Inquisition where the executioner raised his sword and simply split my head like it was a gourd, and to a musket ball between the eyes as a dashing lieutenant in the army of the South (Hood's Texicans to be more precise) during our Civil

War. These regressions showed me the thought patterns that needed to be erased to free me. Again let me say that it worked! Haven't had a headache of any kind in many years. Now I'd better give you the "How to."

A simple technique for examining past lives by yourself

We also study time as a dimension, and the possibility of dimension shift to go forward as well as backward in time. It does work reasonably well even for going forward—someday maybe in time to see tomorrow's lottery results so you can buy a winning ticket before the drawing. But let's table that notion and get to how to look for specific problems that have come forward from past lives.

The idea is to break loose from the confines of time as most of the world accepts it. We use a process of visualization that the world would tend to put down as imagination. Let's not quibble about terminology, but just use it. So sit or lie comfortably somewhere where you're not too apt to be disturbed. Breathe slowly and deeply for awhile to help set the mood. Then begin to shrink your consciousness until you become a tiny dot between your eyes. (It's an interesting sensation when well visualized; you can feel the detachment from the floor, chair, etc., and be very tiny!) Next you expand your consciousness to fill the whole room. *Feeling* it is the key. Then shrink again to that tiny dot behind your eyes (if you were to shrink any more you would find yourself in the Zen Void, but save that for another exercise and just be content to be tiny). Again expand your consciousness, this time to fill the whole city. Follow by shrinking again to be that tiny dot. Then this time expand to fill the whole planet and while you're in that expanded state, float upward high enough to break your connection with time and space, then settle back down to be in the time period of your choice. Look down at your body to see what you're wearing, then take in the surroundings and your daily activities, etc. And ask to see the situation that caused you to have the problem in your current life. It works quite easily. With my migraines I kept getting visions for a couple of hours after I asked the question—so don't be impatient, just expect to see enough to understand and thus overcome the problem in the here and now. Usually you can just decide that you're back in the here and now, but if you seem stuck, just float back up to break the connection and then settle gently back into your body. This is a gentle and very practical use of the out-of-body experience which is most often called *astral projection*. And you can use it safely at any time—just remember to always float up into Light.

More uses for the astral realms

Our earlier work on shifting dimensions paid off in many ways. In early 1984, spirit prompted us to move the E.S.P. Lab from the hustle and bustle of Los Angeles to the peaceful East Texas countryside where we are today. The new facility had far less room than the big building we enjoyed in L.A. so it became a lesson in downsizing by transferring much of our gadgetry from the physical to the astral realms. Surprisingly they all work better from there! Remember, the circuit diagrams worked as well as the actual physical radionics devices, and when our visualization processes improve with practice, they will work better yet. After you get used to your physical pyramid, you'll be able to transfer it to the astral, too, for faster and more convenient results. We'll get to that "how to" as soon as we get your Spirit Party going joyously.

The lessons in downsizing continued right along until mid 1997 when my physical altar (that I had used personally since the early 1950s) got destroyed. I sat down at my desk feeling completely devastated, but Pan quipped at me: "Forget it, Al, you don't need that anymore, let it stay on the astral." And indeed all my ritual work for people around the world is working better than ever before. When we've outgrown a "crutch," so to speak, spirit has its ways of removing it almost painless-ly. There is always a lesson in spiritual–psychic growth in any apparent tragedy and, if we grab it, we come through much stronger and more effective than before.

In metaphysical terms, any tragedy has good in it some-where. Think of it as a small tree and shake it until the good falls down in front of you. This will work for you, every time you use it!

Hey! Let's get back to at least starting the party

According to Pan and Puck, and the friendly Nature Spirits they "preside over," *work* is the most repulsive four-letter word in the English language. This little quip is one of my favorites: "Find a job you like and you'll never have to work another day of your life." For instance, I put on a special seminar in Wash-ington, D.C., over Labor Day weekend, 1998. We billed it as a super Spirit Party and there was no "work" at all involved in doing it. The times I was on camera were the most fun for me—many years ago that sort of thing was what I called a dreaded form of work. The difference is simply attitude and the confidence that comes from well-established camaraderie with one's own special Spirit People.

Another important idea behind our Spirit Party concept is that you no longer have to beg or pray for help from a distant, perhaps a bit blurry, God. Dr. Rhine gave us the best clue—humor is the catalyst for all forms of E.S.P. It's also a wonder-ful thing to share as a way to generate camaraderie with your Spirit Friends. Then you don't have to beg for guidance and/or tangible help. Friends enjoy helping friends especially when your request is: "Hey, guys, wouldn't it be fun if we . . ." Think of it like the old days when they had barn-raising parties. Everybody had a good time and the barn got built. We'll get to how to start and perpetuate your Spirit Party in a little while. Meanwhile let's look at what follows.

Spirit Party games can include winning the lottery, casino gambling, bingo, and whatever you like

In June 1997 we decided to add a "Lottery Program" to our ongoing E.S.P. Lab Spirit Party. Let's share a bit of feedback from a participant or two:

> "I got three numbers in the New York Take-Five Lottery successively on the 11th, 12th, 16th, 19th, and 29th of last month, followed by the three on the 2nd, 16th, and 17th, then the 23rd and 24th of this month. Pretty good lottery program performance!" —*L. S., New York*

Every once in awhile he gets four numbers as well.

> "I'm so happy to report that I received four numbers from the Take-Five drawing. Here's Spirit's share, $46.40. Sincere thanks." —*L. S., New York*

He's been doing this consistently from July 1997 through September 1998. O.K., not making a big fortune, but super fun entertainment that pays you to play. I'd guess he's netted about $100/week over the 14-month period. The fun is even more rewarding as is the possibility of a big win, and it enhances the camaraderie with spirit. Since he was doing a little better at it than I, I asked him how he did it. This was his response:

> "You asked me to share the details of my extraordinary success in the lottery program. Twice a day, at night before I retire and in the morning when I arise, I approach my altar and give thanks and request the protection of Mother Isis. I pick my numbers at random and purchase the ticket at an Isis hour. It seems to work all the time. Sincere thanks." —*L. S., New York*

The reference to the Isis hour comes from the planetary hours system given in my *White Witchcraft* book we mentioned earlier. Have a look if it interests you. Meanwhile, how about sharing a couple more feedback letters:

> "My second video 'Loving & Laughing Your Way to Better & Better Everything with Spirits' made my purse happy! I played the Power Ball Wednesday and won $7. Friday I played my tape—my spirits were lifted so high I played a three-digit and boxed for a dollar and won $580! Saturday I won $11 on the Power Ball!" —*W. M., West Virginia*

> "Thanks for the energy and good thoughts you sent our way while in Las Vegas. A and I kept winning small jackpots and it kept our day very pleasant and easygoing. You are so wonderful and needed. Thank you." —*P. S., Texas*

> "The Lottery program is working (3) small wins, heading for the big winners now. Here's my donation. Sincerely." —*J. H., Missouri*

Now the Spirit Party "how to"

This is chapters 10 and 11 carried to the next level. You've met many of your spirit guides, teachers, and friends on a more or less formal basis. Now it's time to make it all FUN—if it's fun for you, it will indeed be fun for your Spirit People. And the camaraderie we produce this way will provide the energy for everything you might dream of accomplishing. Dream might be a good word for this part of the unfolding, but visualization or the upbeat meaning of imagination will do nicely.

First, if you haven't yet adopted my pet motto/rule for life ("If I can't have a good time, I'm not going"), do it now! And understand that your Spirit People already live that way. So let's declare a permanent Spirit Party à la that magnificent old musical, *Guys and Dolls,* and the "Oldest established, reliable, permanent floating crap game in New York." Take a glass or cup of your favorite beverage to your altar or meditation place, relax, and lift it as a toast to all the Spirits and Nature Spirits around you. Call as many by name as you can this first time and say something like: "Hi, my good friends, Well-Come to our party. Let's declare this a permanent part of our lives and share it together all day and night, always." A little singing of some sort is always nice to get a party rolling. Let me suggest a nice song of thanks to the tune of *Silver Bells:*

> Verse: Pretty flowers, loving people sharing joy all day long, a wonderful life to be living. Lots of money, health, and beauty always coming my way, thanksgiving is all I can say.

> Chorus: Thank you, Pan, Abraxas, Bast. Thanks, Ishtar, Puck, Thoth, and Isis. Thanks, Marduk, Nergal, Ra, all good things are coming my way.

Well, you need to thank somebody—the spirits we thank in that chorus are mostly people we met while writing the *White Witchcraft* book. If you're not familiar with them, you will be after you sing to them a few times. And how about writing a verse or two of your own and sharing them with us. For that, or if you're having any problems getting your attunements, please get to me by phone, regular mail, fax, e-mail, or try my website: www.vzinet.com/esplab. I'll give you all the numbers at the close of this chapter. The name of the game is *enjoy and win!*

How to transfer your pyramid and other magickal gadgetry to the astral and make them even more effective

Let's quote Pan again about the destruction of my altar: "Forget it, Al, you don't need that anymore, let it stay on the astral!" All it takes is an enlightened decision. That's easy because we know now that the energy of manifestation is the enthusiasm/love energy you generate so nicely at your Spirit Party, and the thoughtform is your clear mental–emotional picture of your desired outcome.

O.K., it's time to quit talking about it, make the decision that your pyramid is now astral, and get to the doing. Always have your number-one immediate goal clearly pictured when you start. Reach out to Abraxas, feel his loving, chuckling response, and call on your own Spirit People, all our TexLab Spirits, and Astral Al, too. Tell us you want to cuddle, wallow in the wonderful love, and feast with us on the ambience. *Feel* loved through and through. Bask in it, wallow in it, and let it fill you with confidence and a delightful sense of well-being. Savor it, there's plenty of time to get practical. The deeper you feel the love, the better all of life will go for you.

When you feel marvelously ready, picture the end result of your number-one goal, fill it with the delightful love you're now enjoying, and tell it it's time to delightfully manifest *now*. It will believe you and do it very soon.

How often should you enjoy this happy exercise? As often as you like for one intention or goal at a time, just so long as you keep it fresh and new. Do wallow in the love with all of us and win some real biggies *now!*

What kind of results should you expect from your ongoing Spirit Party?

Just a little over five years ago, we adopted a secondary motto for the Lab. The original motto which we still adhere to 100 percent is: "RESULTS!" The secondary motto is: "Everything getting ever better and better with *no* upper limit." For over five years we've been making this work, and the results are magnificent. Let's just borrow a few quotes from the November 1998 E.S.P. Lab of Texas Newsletter as a nice "for instance":

> "I asked for your help getting a new job—got it! Asked for treatment for a good start—got it! Now how about giving me a once-a-month candle ritual for the next three months for business and job success." —*R. G., Pennsylvania*

"Great news! After almost a year of waiting, I've finally received the very important document which had been stolen from me. I guess the second modified candle ritual did the trick! Please accept this donation for E.S.P. Lab for all the great work you and Spirits have done for me. It's really a great feeling to know that besides the rising sun, there is something else which I can really rely on—you and E.S.P. Lab! Fantastic work, guys! I don't know how I'd live this life without you guys! Thanks, thanks, thanks a million again!" —*K. E., Mahe, Seychelles*

"My loss of too many close friends lately and too many aches and pains have somewhat lowered my old constant joy and enthusiasm which I know are essential to successful living. (In spite of many small setbacks, I recouped quickly.) So I'm working at gaining much joy in life again and asking Spirit help in my ritual work. And Spirit helped amusingly at my Ritual of Joy. Music always meant joy to me, so I tried to recall my years in a great choral group (in Hollywood, CA)—no dice. Going further back I'd taped with piano recording, gaily trilling. No dice, no fun. So— further back in years I recalled 'Party Time'—great fun dance music banging along gaily. More like it! I grew very happy. And the music sounded very familiar. As it should have! I played for dances countless times back then! A vigorous merry, jazz-swing type piano. The lovely, merry 'concert' kept playing in my head. Fun time again, my playing up a storm! Spirit had answered my request for a revival of happiness. As you know, Spirit knows everything and can do anything!" —*M. H., Texas*

"Thanks so much for everything through the 18 years of my Lab membership! It means a lot—I put things I have learned into practice every day and the miracles are too many to count. Please accept my renewal of membership for the year and congratulations on your new 35-year cycle. Light, love, and laughter!" —*S. R., Colorado*

"A week or so ago I received your book about the magick of the White Unicorn. Have read it through, finding it most interesting, and now am studying it. And it goes slowly because some of it is most difficult to grasp, though I understand most of it. After reading a few pages I saw a Unicorn prancing in front of me. A true surprise so I welcomed him. He was and is happy and is perched on my left shoulder. Then one evening as I was about to fall asleep I saw a smiling face that I'm sure was Bast. Am working to eliminate the old karma. Keep up the good work, Al." —*H. O., California*

POINTS TO REMEMBER

I. Your E.S.P. can solve major problems and lead you to wonderful fresh opportunities.

II. Dr. Rhine helped establish the value of humor in E.S.P. applications.

III. Orgone force, Odic force, and Pyramid energy are worthy of your attention.

IV. Pyramid-assisted thoughtform building can bring major positive changes for you.

V. There are practical uses for the study of your own past lives.

VI. You can examine your past lives by yourself.

VII. Time is a dimension that can be used both forward and backward.

VIII. Party games with Spirit can bring you an ever better and better life.

IX. Let's get in touch and play together to make all of our lives ever better and better with no upper limit. *And let's stay in touch!*

My first 9 books were for Prentice Hall—I now have a total of about 23 books, all of which I think you should have. There are a good 33 years of lore and progress waiting for you. Do start with *Helping Yourself with White Witchcraft* but don't stop there. Spirit and I want you to get on the bandwagon and play with us at E.S.P. Lab of Texas. Do write, call, fax, e-mail, or at least visit our website at www.vznet.com/esplab. Our mailing address is PO Box 216, Edgewood, TX 75117; phone number is 903-896-1700; fax number is 903-896-7770; and e-mail address is <astralal@vzinet.com>. Let's play together NOW!

Index

A

Accidents, 41–42
  consciousness of accident
    prone, 41–42
  protection from harm exer-
    cise, 77–78
  protection of spirit guides,
    37, 95–96
Achievement
  and occultism, 40
  and peace of mind, 115
Altar, 163
Ancestor worship, 133
Angels, religious context, 30–31
Antimatter, 173
Anxiety, interference with sub-
    conscious, 13, 23, 24,
    157
Apports, 154–55
Arjuna, 132, 134
Ascended masters, 33
Asking, benefits of, 78–79
Astral travel, 14, 154
Atoms, 173
Aura
  and attraction in relation-
    ships, 82–83, 91
  and healing, 50, 56–57
  seeing aura, 49–50, 158–59,
    180
  size and scope of, 49
  thoughtforms in, 180
Aura vision, seeing visiting
    spirits, 145–46
Automatic writing, 146
Awareness, relaxed awareness,
    5, 23, 42

B

Balance
  achievement of, 175
  importance of, 17, 139–40
  psychic exercise for develop-
    ing, 18–19
Bannister, Roger, 26
Bhagavad-Gita, 132, 134
Bible, accounts of E.S.P., 25
Billet reading, 153–54
Breathing exercise, for relax-
    ation, 26
Brow Center, purpose of, 17
Buddha, 111–12
Burbank, Luther, 39

Important Pages

P. 26